VIET JOURNAL

By James Jones

VIET JOURNAL

James Jones

A DELTA BOOK

To Fred and Arline Weyand
for Obvious Reasons.

And to The United States Army
To Which My First Novel
Was Also Dedicated.

A DELTA BOOK
Published by
Dell Publishing Co., Inc.
1 Dag Hammarskjold Plaza
New York, New York 10017

Portions of this book appeared in the following: *The New York Times Magazine, Harper's,* and *Oui.*

For information address Delacorte Press, New York, New York.
ISBN: 0-385-29426-3
Reprinted by arrangement with Delacorte Press
Printed in the United States of America
First Delta printing — September 1985

Acknowledgments

I want to thank newsmen of *The New York Times* Saigon bureau, in particular Charles Mohr, Henry Kamm, and Sylvan Fox, for their help and advice to a newcomer. Thanks also to Hugh Mulligan, Dick and Toby Pyle, and the AP bureau in general for their kindness, generosity, and sense of humor. My appreciation also to Col Robert Burke, US Army. Finally I want to thank especially warmly Joe Treaster of the *Times* bureau and his wife, Barbara, who took me into their home and under their wing.

Nor can I finish without a sincere thank-you to Bob Wool and Lew Bergman of *The Sunday Times Magazine*, who wet-nursed the whole project from the beginning.

The Call

I've been known to say over the years—usually when in my cups—that had I not opted to become a writer, I'd have stayed in the Army, acquired a commission, and been a career soldier.

Advancing middle age does strange things to men. In January of 1942 my father went around to the nearest recruiting station and tried to volunteer for a commission in the Infantry, as a lieutenant. He was 56 at the time, a known alcoholic, a mediocre vet of World War I, and a failure at his profession of dentist. The Army turned him down. Cold. They didn't even want him as a dentist. He wrote me a rather despairing letter about it. I read it, wondering how he could imagine the Army would want him for anything. At the time I was on a beach position in Honolulu, a corporal of Infantry myself. Before that spring was out, my father was to commit suicide by shooting himself in the head. Later I would speculate often whether that turndown by the Army had not been such a slap in the face that it helped awaken him to what he was, what he had become, and he could not stand to face it. I loved my father, and I hated to see it end like that. He deserved a better fate.

Over the long years of the Vietnam War I had always been against sending a large US Army there. Particularly a draftee Army, in which the soldier had no right to say "Yes" or "No." I would not have minded so much a recruited Army of volunteers, who knew what they were getting. I was against European or American colonialism in the area, but I had no great love for the North Vietnamese, either. I would not have liked to live in their society. Over the years I had been asked two or three times to go out there and write about the war, and had always declined. Mainly because I could not see getting my ass shot off, over Vietnam. Partly because I was cynical about both sides, including US involvement. So I went ahead with my life, and my work, trying to steer between the fanatics on both sides.

The first call came sometime in mid-January, 1973, from a Mrs. Lazar who was the *New York Times Magazine* stringer in Paris. If I was interested, I should call a Mr. Robert Wool in New York. I called Wool that afternoon. Wool laid it out for me. They wanted me to go out there and write up for them what it was like, after the cease-fire. "The sights, the sounds, the smells of Vietnam—after the end." That sounds funny now. "I'm not political," I said. They didn't want a political, they had hundreds of those to send. They wanted a "novelist's viewpoint." "A Novelist's Journal." I could feel my pulse speeding up. They would pay me X dollars a piece for one, or two pieces. They would pay expenses. It wasn't much money. But I could always get a book out of the trip, too, Wool said. They wanted me to go to both North Vietnam and South Vietnam. They would take care of the visas, and all that.

"To both?" I said.

Absolutely, both. They would handle the visas. I found the idea of going to both a lot more enticing.

Take a day or two to think it over, and call him back, Wool said.

I hesitated. I had just finished a "thriller" novel, which was coming out, and that was out of the way. But I was just starting back to work on a big novel, one I had put aside twice, to do something else. As I said, advancing middle age does strange things to men. I told Wool I would call him back, and put the phone down gently as if it might break in my hand, or bite me.

Doubts

They started coming right away.

First I had to find out what my wife thought. And, naturally, she was almost certainly going to be against it. She was. What could anybody my age, who was not a reporter, and who had not been around any dangerous shooting for thirty years, possibly want in Vietnam? But she was pretty good about it. I cast around, trying to analyze why I wanted to go. Finally, I said I wanted to go because I was fifty-two. She nodded at that. I would probably never get another chance at an adventure like this, I went on. In a few years, one more novel perhaps, and I would be too old for it. She nodded again. I don't know what was going on down in the deep bottom of her mind. But she said, go. I knew how hard it was for her to say it. We had only been separated a couple of times for a few days in fifteen years.

So her objections were out of the way. But other demurrers began to rise up, steadily, regularly, one by one. What could I possibly write about Vietnam that hadn't already been written?

All I knew about Vietnam was what I had more or less been forced to read in the daily papers. The whole thing was such a colossal fiasco for America— if I could believe what the papers said—that I had tried to avoid thinking about it.

After World War II I had detested politics, and politicians. That is not to say I imagined we could get along without them. But I had never seen a politician whose personal ambition did not come first, before his desire to help humanity. Politicians were people who either had too much money, or not enough. Either way, they went into politics because they lacked the talent or the guts to succeed in a decent profession. That they often wound up working harder in politics than they would have in a decent profession, was beside the point.

If this was perhaps a heartless view, I had seen nothing much in the intervening years to make me change my mind.

But that we were becoming the new fascists, in America? I could not believe that. A lot of the foreign press was calling us that. A lot of our own press, in a kind of moral hysteria, was taking up the same cry, without much discrimination.

We were still a nation of Puritans—still hungering after that same Plymouth purity that had never existed, except in some half-baked theory.

On the other hand, I knew of no other nation that would allow its press to come out in full attack against the good faith of its government. Certainly not North Vietnam. And not South Vietnam.

Granting that we were wrong in Vietnam, the problem was how far wrong were we. Granting that we had failed, how far had we failed? And why? Had we failed because we were fascist, were morally evil? A lot of people were trying to prove that. I had never seen a defeated US Army. Did I really want to?

Were we really in danger of becoming a military-industrial dictatorship? Was the Army really a collection of sadistic fascist redneck killers? It had changed a lot since my day. Had it changed that much? Did I really want to find out?

I was not sure I did. But I called Wool in New York next day and told him I would go. I did not even wait the two full days. Something else a lot more powerful than politics was working in me, that sense of encroaching age and a last adventure, telling me to go.

The Preparation

Preparing for a trip is likely to be the best part of it. Of course if you knew that beforehand you probably wouldn't go. And then the preparation wouldn't mean anything. I suspect half the voyages made are made, finally, so we can say in honesty afterward that we have been some place.

For a week I ran around Paris in a kind of jaw-clenched, eye-crossed dead run, preparing. I was like a kid in a candy shop. A lot of it had to do with getting shots. There was an unbelievable number of them to get. I became the best shot-getter in the history of the American Hospital of Paris. I had every shot it was possible to get into the WHO yellow booklet, except yellow fever. I begged my doctor to give me that too, though there was no yellow jack in Vietnam, so that I could have a grand slam; but he refused. The two cholera shots, a week apart, knocked me out for two days apiece. The smallpox vaccination, though I had had one three years before, took anyway. I was a walking collection of sores and sore spots. I believed I could actually have gone swimming in the Seine without ill effects or falling ill.

Getting the bubonic plague shot was interesting. Bubonic was one of the optionals. But I was advised to take it. Getting someone to give it to me, however, posed quite a problem. Nobody had the serum or knew where to get it. My own doctor didn't have it, and none of the airlines had it or knew where to find it. Finally after ten phone calls and several fruitless taxi rides all over Paris, I ran the serum to earth at the Pasteur Institute in their Department of Tropical Medicine. A reluctant Dr. Mollaret there had it in his icebox, and would give it to me if I could catch him between classes, which was next to impossible he warned me. In his cluttered dusty office packed with dusty files, tropical medicine tomes, and bound students' papers, he broke off attacking some wan emaciated med student and gave me a brilliant smile, and keeping up an explosive highly colored recitation on the horrors of Far East diseases which he had studied all over the East, danced over to his dilapidated refrigerator and got out his serum. This he drew off into an old just-boiled glass hypodermic the size of a Model T Ford's cylinder, through a needle the size of your grandma's knitting stick, and plunged the needle into my shoulder muscle beside my neck. The pain was excruciating. My doctor had warned me about old-fashioned methods at the Institute, so I kept my eyes on the window and remembered not to clench my teeth so my jaw muscle would not ripple. The wan med student stared at me with interest. Dr. Mollaret withdrew the needle and giving me another brilliant smile, patted my shoulder. He had decided I would do, apparently. But I must have another shot, one week hence. If I did not yet have my visas, never fear, I would still be here. I left wanting to laugh at that. The good doctor, however, knew his Far East and their visas far better than I.

But there were sober moments. Riding across to the Right Bank in a taxi through the drizzle, to see about a pair of boots, I was struck by a sense of historical continuity in what I was doing. Paris was so gray and rainy and cold in January. How many imperialists, how many missionaries—how many men, had gone around Paris in the winter drizzle, collecting a tropical outfit to take South with them? Empire-builder had not been a bad word to them. Then history had moved on.

The signing of the accords came and went, with my having hardly noticed. Rogers and Kissinger arrived and left without my seeing them. The cease-fire would begin January 28th. The Americans would be out of Vietnam sixty days after, on March 28th.

Visas

In my state of high it had not occurred to me I might have *real* trouble getting visas. In the first flush of enthusiasm over our new love affair, New York had told me they would take care of my visas to both Vietnams for me. As it turned out, the mighty *New York Times* organization was powerless to get me a visa to either. In the end I got my South Vietnam visa myself. I never did get a visa to North Vietnam.

I had half expected trouble from the North Viets, and warned Wool of this. The North Viets were notoriously selfish about visas, preferring to give them to people like Jane Fonda, Wilfred Burchett, and Mary McCarthy, people already strongly on their side, thus harvesting bumper crops of unabashed propaganda from each seedling. Not to worry, was

Wool's answer. In reality, the only resource at Wool's command was to cable Hanoi an official request in the name of the *Times*. This he did, and got back a politely worded negative. This should not upset us, Wool said. It often happened. And then on the second try they would come through like lambs. He would try them again in a week.

Meantime, I was to submit my formal request at the South Vietnam consulate in Paris. Wool would see what he—what the *Times*—could do to help in Washington. The trouble with this was that, what with the official US disinvolvement after the cease-fire, the US State Department had stopped handling visas directly, and had turned all that over to the South Viet Ministry of State. Where it was subcontracted to the Press Ministry. The South Viets, Washington said, were not set up for this kind of an operation, and had no experience at it, and it was making them slow. For a while I accepted this. But as the days, and then the weeks, passed, I began to think there might be a little more to it than that.

The day I went up to the South Viet consulate in the Avenue des Villiers to tender my visa application was the day after the accords were signed. The little townhouse, transformed into a working office by thousands of square feet of ugly plywood partitioning, was swarming with media representatives seeking visas. It was easy to see why there might be a bottleneck in getting one. Handing in my application to the Viet ladies beyond the counter, I ran head-on into a South Viet phenomenon I would encounter often later on. I do not know about the North Vietnamese—but the South Viet men you met and had to deal with, though they were constantly unfailingly polite and almost overconsiderate, were as unbending as steel bars. But when they had a really tough hard mean bitchy job to do, they invariably gave it to the women. The South Viet women were the hardest-minded, most self-focused, self-admiring, grasping acquisitive females I had met since encountering the French. They made short work of me—and the other applicants—at the counter. I, on my side, contented myself with noting the extraordinary number of mink coats hanging on the clerk-force coat racks, the large numbers of diamonds flashing from clerk-force arms and necks. Could they *all* be relatives of politicos? Who accepted clerks' jobs to get out? My visa application was grudgingly accepted, and I was told sharply that I would be informed. The next day I began a long series of almost daily phone calls to a Mr. Quyen, the Press Attaché himself, a man.

I decided to put in some time on the North Vietnamese. Wool's second appeal to Hanoi had gone unanswered. Letters by me to the Paris consulate were not answered. Phone calls never reached the PR man I was trying to get, or anyone else in authority. Everybody was always out.

I had some journalist friends in Paris who had been accepted in Hanoi. I tried enlisting their aid. Mary McCarthy and Olivier Todd, for example, had both been to Hanoi. I asked both for help. Miss McCarthy, an old and dear friend, particularly went way out of her way to help me. But letters and phone calls from Todd and McCarthy were like stones dropped into a well.

I had never written anything against the North Viets that might turn them off on me. I had tried to remain scrupulously neutral on the war. But maybe that in itself was enough to put me on their special blacklist? I began to feel like some kind of undesirable. Each unrequited phone call made me guiltier. Finally, armed with a special letter from Mary McCarthy, I decided to go there in person.

There seemed to me to be a mass national paranoia operating among the North Vietnamese. Phone calls to their consulate were treated with the kind of pinched-face, moral suspicion usually encountered only among middle-western ladies' clubs when the subject of prostitution comes up. Always when you called and gave your name and asked for Mr. Mai, there would be that moment of intent stillness at the other end, before the other party, man or woman, gave his automatic negative. Maybe they were just nervous. I felt that if I could just make one significant human contact, reach just one of them on a personal level, perhaps I could get through to them. Explain I was no capitalist-imperialist pig trying to do them in.

The consulate was on a short little street called rue le Verier. It was a small townhouse like the other, was on the corner, and had a uniformed French cop strolling up and down out in front. Well, the other place had a cop out in front too, hadn't it? It is hard still today to fix a reasonable basis for what followed, whether it was my own paranoia or their paranoia, or both, that caused it. I got out and paid my taxi. The cop on the corner gave me a once-over scrutiny. I tried to look innocent and friendly. I walked up the two steps to the door. Then I made the mistake of trying to open the door. What the hell, the door at the other consulate hadn't been locked? This door was locked. I was surprised, and suddenly felt foolish, then guilty. I would swear the cop took a couple of

steps toward me. Hastily, I rang the doorbell, then
when nothing happened, knocked on the door with
my fist. It was one of those wide double French-style
doors, with a frosted window in each side covered
with ornamental forged-iron grills. Suddenly the
door opened and a blond white man in a leather coat
came out and brushed past me. Then the window in
front of me opened—not the door itself—and a Caucasian woman's face, cold and aggressive with suspicion, appeared in front of mine. What did I want? she
said rudely in French. I immediately felt guilty, and
just as immediately, furious. I had had no chance to
recover from finding the door locked. My voice came
out haltingly: I had a letter. From Miss Mary
McCarthy. For Mr. Mai. I waved the letter. From behind me a big broad white man in a leather coat and
with cropped blond hair, for all the world exactly like
a Russian secret cop, came up the steps, muttered
something to the woman, and half-shouldered me
aside. The woman slipped the door open for him. He
went in. She quickly shut the door. I caught a glimpse
of two Oriental gentlemen in slim Western suits
standing behind her. The woman was telling me in
the rudest, bluntest, most insulting French that Mr.
Mai did not see anyone without an appointment, I
should telephone, she would take the letter. Her tone
was that of a schoolteacher with a child. Sort of
numbly I pushed the letter through the grill. She shut
the window. I had not even got to say I had been
telephoning Mr. Mai for days. Then I realized that the
man who had just gone in was the same man who had
just come out minutes before. What had he been doing? Checking me? Was he some kind of special en-
forcer? Behind me on the sidewalk the French cop

watched me noncommittally. In front the locked door stared back at me. I turned and left. Around the corner I found a normal, familiar, everyday café-tabac— with pinballs, an Italian coffee machine, a red awning, and a mob of long-haired, dirty-jeaned French students trying hard to be insolent. Shaky with fury, and something very like fear, I used the phone booth at the back to call a taxi to take me home. Further phone calls to Mr. Mai produced nothing. My one consulate visit remained the full extent of my personal contact with the North Vietnamese.

Meanwhile, there was no word from the South Viets either. Daily it was coming clearer and clearer that, now that they were running their own show, the South Vietnamese were adopting the same propagandistic attitude toward visas as their Northern cousins.

Body Punching

All this time Wool and I were burning up the transatlantic phone wires, at great expense to the *Times*. I had never met Wool. But over the days and then weeks of visa hunting we had built up a friendship by telephone, cemented by our common anxiety. Wool was one of the younger, livelier editors at the *Times Magazine*. Apparently the whole idea of sending me out had been Wool's baby, along with some of the other younger editors. Now Wool was doing the best he could for me about visas, but there wasn't that much he could do. When the South Viet Embassy in

Washington told him his request had been referred to Saigon—the classic dodge—Wool's only recourse was to turn me over to the *Times* foreign-bureau system. Telex the Saigon bureau to expedite the visa, telephone the Paris bureau to try and help me get it. This was about like turning a spastic mouse—me—over to a quite honorable, but hungry, family of domesticated cats.

The problem, essentially, lay in the fact that the daily *Times* and the *Times Sunday Magazine* were two distinct and autonomous organs. And of the two there was no question which was bigger and the more powerful and swung the most weight. Compared to the daily *Times* with its hierarchy of editors and departments and far-flung, worldwide network of foreign bureaus, the *Magazine* was a pretty weak relative. It seemed this was not talked about, but it was there just the same, and it appeared the daily *Times* was pretty proud and jealous of its priority. In any case, when it came to things like foreign visas and the like—pull, in other words—pull, where it counted— the *Magazine* had to go to Big Brother's news network and systems of bureaus and contacts.

I had no way of knowing what went on in the Saigon bureau when Wool's request arrived—just that Saigon wired back it could be of little help. But from the moment I first walked into the Paris office on the rue Scribe I knew that if I got any visas, it would not be because of the Paris bureau.

I knew, of course, that in any organization there were bound to be secret fights and abrasions the insiders did not talk about before the uninitiated. The bigger the organization, the bitchier and meaner the fights. I also knew that no matter what I did I was going to make enemies, coming in as a nonjournalist. But understanding such an idea intellectually, and seeing it at work in action in front of your face, were two different quantities.

From the second I passed inside the door with its huge polished brass plate reading NEW YORK TIMES, I could smell from the polite disassociation of the receptionist and secretaries that I was an outsider. The hard noncommittal smiles and bright silences of the staffers I met indicated bestselling novelists were no great thing to them and could expect neither aid nor friendship. They were all obviously waiting for me to meet the boss.

There was no question as to who that was. Poor little Mrs. Lazar the *Magazine* representative, out in her one small room in the seldom-visited back recesses of the joint, was not any personage of great weight or import around this office, and nobody however polite was going to let on for my benefit that she was. The boss was the bureau chief.

On the other hand, the well-known staff writers were important figures. The second or third day I was in the office Henry Kamm, the feature writer, came in. Mrs. Lazar had told me he was also waiting for a visa. When he saw me and learned who I was, Kamm refused to meet me, and cut me. I happened to be sitting at his desk, using his desk phone. I got up and went over to him and putting on my most charming smile apologized for using his desk. Later Kamm and I became friendly out in Saigon, and he probably helped me more than any newsman I met out there. But at the moment, he only smiled sourly.

The chief of the Paris bureau was Mrs. Flora Lewis. I had never met Mrs. Lewis. But I had read her pieces for years. And I had seen her on a few French TV shows. She was a striking, handsome woman on TV, and in person apparently she was Big Sister incarnate. She appeared to have her whole staff slightly terrorized. Little Mrs. Lazar, no small ego in her own little office, was scared to death of her. Apparently she ran her outfit like an old-time martinet, with a few added feminine refinements of her own, such as fits of frayed nerves from overwork, and a sort of periodic despair of fatigue, caused by her heavy responsibilities. I was not even able to meet her for the first five days I started coming in to the office. When finally I did, she took me into her private bureau chief's office and explained—with great patience for someone so overworked—that while she sympathized with my worries over getting a visa and would do everything she could to help me, I must not expect too much too quickly and must realize she had a great many other, much more important things to occupy her over-stretched time and energy at the present moment. I got the message. I said I understood how overworked she must be, and thanked her. Then I got out of there while I still had my head still on my shoulders instead of in my hands. And went to see what I could do on my own. The answer to which was nothing.

In the ring, a body puncher is distinguished by the way he keeps both shoulders low and by the fact that he almost never goes for the head. He is less spectacular than the knockout-artist head-hitter. But any trainer will tell you he is far more efficient and therefore more dangerous in the long run. Unfortunately for the fight game, but perhaps fortunately for him, he is also the source of most of the serious fouls that occur. After all, it is only about six inches from the groin to the navel. And the body puncher daren't be looking down all the time to check his accuracy. Also, a large percentage of body fouls occur when the referee is not even in a position to see them. Let alone call them. I had fallen in with a whole train of journalistic body punchers, each of whom kept his hand and eye in by constant daily workouts with the others, and I was having difficulty covering up.

I have read that before World War I there were no such things as passports and visas. I find that hard to believe. But I have met people who lived back then and they swear that it is true. It is difficult to imagine a world in which you passed from country to country with your honor and self-esteem intact, uninsulted by bureaucrats, unimpeded by Intelligence freaks, crossing borders in tranquility. The percentage of tourist heart attacks back then must have been dramatically less.

The *Times* was doing nothing. The *Times Magazine* was helpless. I had begun trying to get visas on January 17th. It was now February 23rd. If things kept on, I wouldn't get any visa at all until after the last Americans withdrew March 28th. It is hard to describe the frustration and despair I felt. After deciding to go. After quitting work on my novel. After getting all outfitted and prepared. After taking all the damned shots! Then to be held up indefinitely by politics. The politics—both external, and internal—of getting a visa. I decided to play my one trump card, my only personal ace in the hole. I got on the long-distance telephone and called the wife of General Frederick C. Weyand in Bangkok.

My Friend, the General

I had no idea, when I placed the call, how important knowing Fred Weyand was going to be to my entire Vietnam journey.

Certainly I had no idea how important it was going to be to the getting of my visa. It was simply a shot in the dark. A desperation move. It was Friday, February 23rd, end of the working week, when I talked to Arline Weyand in Bangkok, and told her my trouble. Bright and early Monday morning February 26th, I received a personal phone call from Mr. Quyen the South Viet press attaché. My very first, in fact. My visa was ready and waiting for me at his office. Had been since Saturday morning, but the office was closed. All I had to do was come and pick it up.

I had met the Weyands two years before, in Paris. They turned up at an American-style Thanksgiving dinner party given by my dentist. Fred Weyand, then a lieutenant general, was at the time the American military advisor to the Paris peace talks. He also had commanded the Saigon Military Region in Vietnam during the Tet Offensive of 1968.

My dentist was a rather special case. He had done the teeth of half the movie stars in Europe—including J.-P. Belmondo, Ingrid Bergman, and Deborah Kerr. All of whom were at his party. Years before in Hollywood somebody had asked me if I'd ever noticed that Burt Lancaster, his family, and his friends all had the same smile; and explained that Burt liked his dentist so much he had taken all his family and his friends to him. We were rather like that, at Dr. Marois's. Dr. Marois—Pierre—was also an ardent Americophile. Largely because he adored superior American technology, upon which he was totally dependent in his work. His apartment was equipped with just about every technological gadget on the American market, and looked not unlike the perfect *Playboy* apartment pictured in Hefner's magazine. He gave his American-style Thanksgiving dinner every year, and if you wanted him to keep on working on your teeth so you could go on eating his dinners, you had better show up. Some American friend working for the peace talks delegation had brought the Weyands.

I was drawn to Fred Weyand because he had commanded my old outfit—the 25th "Tropic Lightning" Division. I had been a member of the 25th when it had acquired its nickname, for the fast windup of the campaign on Guadalcanal. Weyand had been a major general when he commanded it in Vietnam in 1965. I had been a private, pfc, corporal, sergeant, and then a private again in it, in that order, in World War II. This difference in rank did not bother either of us. Weyand had read my first, famous novel and then had read the one about Guadalcanal, *The Thin Red Line*, and before the evening was over I found myself telling him in detail the theme for my third Army novel, that I was even then working on, and which with the other two would make a trilogy on World War II and soldiering. It is too complex to go into here, suffice to say it is a quite tragic theme, and when I had finished telling it to him, Weyand's eyes had taken on a kind of inner glow that showed he knew and agreed with exactly what I was driving at. After that we saw quite a bit of each other in Paris, until Weyand was reassigned to Vietnam as second in command to General Abrams. Now, when my visa to Saigon came through, Weyand was a full general and commander of the famous MACV—Military Assistance Command, Vietnam.

I would never have imposed on his friendship if I hadn't been desperate. I had no idea how much my knowing him would affect my Vietnam trip. And I probably wouldn't have imposed on him anyway if it had not been for an American friend of my wife, the wife of a former Israeli ambassador to France who happened to be visiting in Paris. I told her of my hesitancy. Did his wife like me? she wanted to know. I said I thought she did, though she might not like too much some of my outspokenness about sexual matters in my novels. Never mind that, the ex-ambassadress said; is she on your side. I nodded. At least she had invited my wife and me to visit her in Bangkok while she was there. Then call her, my wife's friend said; what do you think the wives of politicians and generals are for?

When I went in to the *Times* office that Monday morning to pick up my expense money, after collecting my visa, it was one of those rare moments of triumph you read about in other people's novels, but never expect to happen to you. The look on the faces of Mrs. Lewis and Mrs. Lazar was worth at least twice the price of the call to Bangkok. Perhaps more.

Departure

It seemed perhaps symbolic that there was a beginning strike on at Orly that morning. Almost no planes were flying. Was I perhaps leaving the declining West, with its tumbling social structures, for the Eastern world of tomorrow?

True to form, little Mrs. Lazar, knowing nothing about the strike, had been unable to do anything about getting me reservations. Fortunately my own travel agent had been on top of it, and had succeeded in getting me a seat on just about the only flight leaving, for Zurich. First Zurich, then Athens, Bangkok, Saigon. There was nobody to see me off. My family, thinking I would already be in Vietnam, had arranged for and then left on an Easter school vacation for the children.

I had been working so hard and playing such games to get a visa, that I had a sudden sobering moment in the cab on the way to Orly. What the hell was I doing here? I had no business here. I would be asking myself the same question, and giving me the same answer, a number of times in the next month. Although it was highly unlikely, it was entirely within the realm of possibility that I could get myself killed, going out to Vietnam like this. As my wife had pointed out. Bob Capa and Bernard Fall had. But at least they had a personal interest. I was no war correspondent.

Nor even a journalist. And I knew nothing at all about Vietnam. I remembered how Wool had delicately suggested insuring me, and I had agreed. For a moment I thought I glimpsed a grinning, chittering face at the back window of the speeding cab, peering in and signaling me.

If I had not been such a coward, I might have turned the cab around right then and gone back home.

The airport at Orly was almost totally deserted. There were not even any porters. I got one of those rolling baskets, and followed a tiny straggling line of passengers down the great empty halls to the checkout for the Zurich plane. We looked forlorn and miniscule in the long echoing corridors.

Arrival

Bangkok prepared me, in a way. Partially. From the air, the flat winding river. The flat steel sheen of flooded rice fields. Off the plane, the soft 7 AM tropic air, full of tropic smells. Stagnant river, burning charcoal, heaped-up garbage. Heaped-up trash, a different, wet-paper odor. Weaving through these like bright threads the scents of the flowers: jasmine, frangipani, bougainvillia, gardenia. The long ride into town from the airport was delicious. A pall of pungent wood smoke floated low over the plain. I stayed a day in Bangkok, and had dinner with Mrs. Weyand, and a thousand sense memories touched me.

The figure that seemed to have followed me here all the way from the taxi outside Orly now seemed to be standing behind each next corner, beckoning, a part of me, waiting to be reconstituted with the rest of me. Hawaii. Fiji. Samoa. New Caledonia. The New Hebrides. The shacks of the poor were like Hawaii in the old days and delightful. The rich cooking smells that came from them, sweet-sour on the tongue, were a potent memory. I had known them, once. As a private soldier in Hawaii, I had lived in them, with a succession of half-Oriental girlfriends. The wraith that seemed a night part of me kept moving back from the next corner, then back from the next. I could never quite catch him face to face.

Saigon was different in its state-of-war situation, and in the fact that Tan Son Nhut airport was closer to the city. The big 707s and 747s from out of the country, touching down momentarily, looked out of place here. Dun military fixed-wings and helicopters rested themselves in protective revetments. Tall sandbag and wire emplacements towered everywhere, their guns leaning against the sky. Outside the airport entrance, all public buildings and military quarters were festooned with wire and armed guards and wrapped around with sandbags. The result of the Tet Offensive in 1968. For me it was still another memory: Honolulu, 1942.

Outside the airport you were immediately in the swarm and motor explosion of the city, consisting mainly of myriads of Hondas, bicyclettes and bicycles, and uncountable numbers of tiny, dented, home-painted, blue and yellow pre-war Citroëns which served as taxis. The car that took me into the city slowed and honked and darted among them like a broken field runner. We passed a tall, ugly, red-brick cathedral. Then a sort of park, with trees and some Buddhist shrines and an incongruously modern, acoustical, speaker's platform, recently constructed, obviously for band concerts—or political speeches. Under tall pleasant shade trees that lined a filthy, dusty sidewalk the car deposited me at the crowded swarming noisy door of the Continental Palace Hotel. I was already sweating profusely.

The lobby was a swarm of foreign newsmen. After I unpacked, I walked the block and a half over to the *Times* office. The cease-fire had been on a month. But there was still heavy fighting in the Central Highlands in the north around Pleiku and Kontum. Villages in the Mekong Delta were still being hit with mortar fire every night. The first POW exchange had gone through, though. And was still the main newsworthy topic of talk. The Americans still had a month to go before their final pull-out, assuming that all went well. At that precise particular moment, nobody was assuming that. There was still an eleven o'clock curfew in Saigon itself.

I found the curfew exciting. By ten-thirty the streets of Saigon began to be deserted. Somewhere overhead a plane would rumble across going North, then another, bombers heading into Tay Ninh or Bien Hoa "after VC." An occasional faint rumble of artillery rounds going in somewhere would come from north of the city. At five of eleven the warning siren went off, eerie over the town, and there would be a last-minute flurry of Hondas and a car or two. A solitary walker would pass unhurried under the tall streetlamps on the central square with its atrocious statue. Then emptiness again. Somewhere off on a

building the siren would wind down in a lonely way.
A small whirlwind of patrolling jeeps would scurry
by like a file of bugs. The white, hot goosenecks went
on burning over the empty square. After a while one
solitary jeep rolled by, checking. But the streets were
empty. Deserted. Every night that I was there, I
watched this ritual from my hotel room window, or
standing in the huge double doors downstairs in the
lobby.

Mr. Conrad and Mr. Maugham

You could sort of smell them both, all over the place.
In the hotel. In the heat-burnt square. In the foul
streets. In the beggars by the door, and the whores on
the terrace. Conrad was never in Saigon. It did not
matter. It is claimed that Mr. Maugham stayed in the
Continental Palace, just as it is claimed that Conrad
stayed at the old Oriental in Bangkok. Actually, when
Conrad was in Bangkok, while taking over command
of the *Otago,* he stayed on board his ship. Because of
a cholera epidemic. And if Mr. Maugham ever stayed
in Saigon, he almost certainly stayed at the Majestic,
a tall old hotel down on the river where nobody stayed
any more as far as I could tell.

But both men are so associated with the Orient.
Conrad in his deeply penetrating brooding way, Mr.
Maugham with his upper-class British colonial snob-
bism. I suspect Mr. Maugham was always a frustrated rubber planter at heart, ordering obedient na-

tive laborers about. Somewhere in his work Conrad writes a vivid picture of two ship's officers sitting on a hotel veranda smoking "cheroots" and looking out over a broad Eastern river. Around them the inscrutable East moves in its unfathomable ways about its mysterious affairs. He does it almost in passing, a throw-away, but the picture stays vividly in the mind as a portrait of the Orient for anyone who has read it. Well, today the East was not so inscrutable. It turned out they wanted the same things as everybody else. Even so, in Saigon, you expected the stooped, full-bearded figure to appear around every corner, the shrewd eyes watching all the Hondas and jeeps perceptively and keeping their own counsel.

Continental Palace

A Vietnamese in a white uniform sits on a stool beside the huge arched wooden doors that are flung wide in the daytime to let in the air. He is there mainly to keep the beggars out of the lobby, and to run errands. Four Vietnamese clerks in white shirts and dark ties sit behind the tall reception desk, scribbling eternally sets of figures in huge ledgers, when not answering the queries of guests. From the high ceiling fans turn lazily, stirring the air. A steep long flight of stairs with a faded red carpet leads up to a decrepit elevator beside which sits a tiny Vietnamese elevator boy in white and a red sash, when he remembers the sash, on another stool. The three upper floors of rooms form a block with windows on the square. All their doors open onto an open corridor along the back, like a cloister, overlooking a banyan-shaded breakfast garden below. In the mornings, the slanting sun throws bright images across the worn yellow tiles down the length of the open corridor.

At night the Viet servant who takes care of the floor you are on sleeps on a pallet on the worn tiles of the corridor. That would be enough to make me a Viet Cong, right there. I always wondered if my floor man was.

I guess the place was famous even before Graham Greene wrote about its terrace. The terrace sits on the corner, buried right back into the building block, under the body of the hotel. Reading Greene, I always thought the terrace was out in the open under the sky. In the "old days," the terrace was a place for the elite to have a cooling drink on a hot afternoon. Nowadays, with the disintegration, it was a hangout for the young hookers, who have no place else to go since the American soldiers left and the bars along Tu-Do Street closed. Nowadays, the girls bring their small children to work with them. The little girls run around and play on the terrace, while mom tries to drum up some trade. I never saw any boy children with them. And I never saw any that looked half Caucasian.

My room was on the top floor. Number 62. They had had a hard time getting it for me. The hotel was perpetually smothered in newsmen from all over. It was *the* place for newsmen to stay. Bob Shaplen had a room in perpetuity on the second floor, which was kept for him even when he was out of the country. Anyone who stayed there had to be prepared to move

27

if Shaplen came to town. A few newsmen like Gavin
Young and Hugh Mulligan rebelled against this
media chic and stayed at other hotels. Like most, my
room was big, cool, lofty, shuttered against the sunlight, with a creaky air-conditioner in one French
window. A ceiling fan turned slowly overhead. The
worn, well-mopped tile floor was wonderfully cool to
the bare feet on a white-hot afternoon. Shabby, faded,
worn, it was solid and Victorian, and therefore comforting. In a country afloat and adrift on a civil war,
it became a haven for me, that room. But I had to keep
it, and pay for it, all the time, even when I went up-
country, or I would lose it.

Franchini

I had been told in Paris to look up M. Franchini, the
owner of the Continental. Very interesting character.
I waited a couple of days. All the while trying hard to
learn the ropes faster than was really possible. When
I asked for him, I was approached by a languid slender sloe-eyed young man who had been loafing in a
chair across the lobby, arguing something explo-
sively with a French correspondent. Franchini had
nothing to do with the running of his hotel. He only
owned it. It was run for him by an urbane rotund
imperturbable half-Chinese gentleman, who needed
no help from anyone. Neither spoke any English.
Franchini occupied himself with his paintings, and
his Chinese lessons, and talked to people in his hotel.

Half Corsican, half Viet himself, he had inherited his hotel from his Corsican father and was married to a pretty Chinese girl from Cholon, and had a two-year-old daughter he doted on like a Corsican.

Franchini was my first real contact with Vietnam. For a man like me, who had no worthwhile contacts, and did not appear likely to make any soon, he was a big help and I spent a large part of my first few days talking to him. He was something of a philosopher, and had cohesive, interlocking sets of ideas about almost everything. The fundamental thread tying it all together was a sort of cheerful despair of humanity. As a race we were bound to end badly. Meantime, Franchini would enjoy himself, and living, if he could. It was he who first advanced me the theory that Viet men were bound to fight, were dedicated to it, just to get away from their women. Franchini believed the Viet women were the tough ones, and as proof put forward the fact it was the women who handled all the really important things like business, and money, and the rapacious social status, and whatever hard work there ever was to be done. While the men, historically always warriors, played politics and soldiering and killed each other. The reason for this was that the Vietnamese had been a conquered people for so much of their history, and the men had lost power and respect. Being a conquered people also accounted for their labyrinthine convoluted way of doing things. I asked him if he thought his theory applied to the North Viets as well. He said he did not know, but he saw no reason to think differently. He said he believed the Northern Communists would probably win, in the end. I asked him why he stayed on, then. He shrugged. Then he said he had many ancestors buried here. I asked him why he allowed the young hookers to turn his terrace into a hangout and place of business. He shrugged again, then said they had nowhere else to go.

During those first disoriented days, when it began to look as if I would never get outside the city limits of Saigon, not at least until it was all over, Franchini and his weird low-key sense of humor kept me from biting myself and giving up.

Hookers and Hookees

The hookers had about ruined Franchini's terrace for anything like tranquil drinking, or a social cocktail with friends. Yet they never accosted you. They waited for you to come to them. I don't know if they had some special deal worked out to that effect with Franchini, or what. I doubt if any of them was much over twenty. They sat two and three at a table and talked a lot, and there was much coming and going between tables. There were always two or three tables of lean-faced hard-eyed young boys, their owner-managers I supposed, keeping an eye on them, and there was a lot of rough horseplay among the boys. The girls themselves had set faces and watchful eyes; but when you got to know them, they laughed a lot and seemed rather happy-go-lucky types, considering. Their customers, the hookees I dubbed them, nowadays were mainly big burly construction workers. Who looked far too big and heavy for the slight, physically delicate Viet girls. When one hookee sat down alone, he was generally set-faced and guilty-looking, hiding his discomfort under a hard poker face. When two or more sat down together, their Protestant-Catholic, Christian American guilt was covered up with a kind of brutal raucous badinage and dirty-sounding laughter. It was as though the more carefree Eastern girls had learned their set hard facial expressions from the customers they served, in trying to be what the Westerners expected of them. Yet the Buddhist East was known to be at least as hard on amateur or professional promiscuity as the Christian West. Between the two, I preferred the hookers to the hookees any time.

At night in the last half hour before curfew, girls who had not found an all-night trick were carried around on the backs of expensive Hondas by their boyfriends from hotel to hotel. Always it was the boy who called out to you as you stood in the hotel doorway. Some nights I would cheerfully wave away as many as ten or twelve motorcycles before the warning siren blew. Always they would wave back as cheerfully and move on. The din from all the revving motors was deafening.

Getting Out of Saigon

Wool and I had decided on four things I would do out there to base articles on. I would go up to Pleiku and Kontum, where there was still serious fighting. I would go out with an ICCS (International Commission of Control and Supervision) team on a field investigation. I would observe a truce violation incident firsthand. And I would cross over and visit a VC or North Viet village or camp. All very neat, and all very organized. All very logical. Poor naive Wool, and poor naive Jones. It wasn't like that at all, when you arrived on the scene. It was neither neat, nor organized, nor logical. I should have remembered that about a war. Only afterward, when the historians start piecing it together, does it become neat and organized and logical, and understandable. Or when newsmen write home about it, and try to make it understandable to their readers.

The day I arrived was the day the North Viets had refused to hand over the second POW list. Newsmen were running around in a flap and making dire predictions about the immediate outbreak of full-scale war again. I did not know then that newsmen have to convince themselves of the validity and immediate contemporary importance of what they write, before they can write it at all. One of the occupational side effects of this is that they lived in a constant state of gloom and unhealthy excitement which was very hard on the nerves. Newsmen are a little like the Hollywood PR propagandists, who create a Marilyn Monroe and then find that they themselves, as well as the current Miss Monroe, have come to believe their own fabrications, trapped by their own myth. In any case, certainly, nobody had time for a snooty novelist who didn't know his thumb from a bull fiddle to come marching in.

Nobody was actively bitchy to me at the bureau office, as in Paris. Or even passively bitchy. It was just that they were all preoccupied with their own rackets. Understandable. I wanted to write something about Vietnam, I'd have to find it for myself. That was fair enough. Since Pleiku-Kontum and the fighting there was one of the main subjects Wool and I had worked out, I asked about that first.

Pleiku was one of the old French mainstays of the Central Highlands. It had long been a major objective of the Viet Minh, and after 1954, of the North Viets and VC. Now it was the South Viet headquarters of MR II—Military Region Two. The famous French outfit *Groupement Mobile 100*, written about so well by Bernard Fall, had fought around there in 1954, and in fact was actually returning there when it met its final ambush by the Viet Minh and ceased to exist as a military unit. There had been heavy fighting going on there and around Kontum twenty-five miles away, continuously since the cease-fire. But when I asked at the *Times* bureau about getting there, I drew blank smiles.

Pleiku was out of the question, I was told. Travel to anywhere was difficult, I learned. Just getting out of Saigon, it appeared, wasn't so easy. Not any more. Not since the Army had gotten recalcitrant and stopped giving rides to newsmen. And nobody was going to Pleiku. Pleiku was a three- or four-day trip by car, normally. But all the roads to it were cut, and cut repeatedly along the route, by the VC and NVA (North Viet Army). Occasionally Air Vietnam sent a plane in, but no one knew just when. I could fly to Hue. But no flights from Hue to Pleiku existed. And even to fly to Hue I would have to wait nine days. All flights were booked solid. And there was no guarantee when I could get back to Saigon.

"Meanwhile, you ought to think about getting an interpreter," the young Viet clerk at the bureau office grinned at me. "I would be glad to arrange for some interviews with interpreters for you."

Another problem I had not faced. I told him to go ahead, and went back to the hotel. I ate lunch with some non-*Times* newsmen I'd met. In the afternoon I interviewed interpreters. I did not find any satisfactory ones. After that I went out and explored Saigon a little. That night I ate an American steak, at a Vietnamese American restaurant, called the Viet-My. It was an affiliate of the Holiday House Hotels. *My* in Vietnamese meant "American." Then I went up to my room alone. And made notes. That became my pattern of life in Saigon for five and a half days. Meantime up north the fighting continued at Kontum. Kontum remained surrounded by the NVA, Highway 14 to Pleiku cut. Pleiku-Kontum, as may be imagined, had become an obsession with me. It looked as though I might go on making notes about Saigon forever.

Garbage

It is a constant presence in Saigon. Everything goes into the street. Early in the morning armies of conical-hatted women with twig witches' brooms and shovels and followed by battered trucks, begin to attack the piles of it. But their hearts are not really in their work and anyway it accumulates faster than they can move it. Old lettuce leaves, the bad parts of tomatoes, the floor sweepings from shops as they open up for the day. The streets are usually slippery with it, so that you have to be careful not to slide and fall. Its variegated aromas are almost visible, and seem to move in colored layers amongst themselves in the super-sun-heated air like a rainbowing oil slick swirling on the waters of a harbor.

It is easy to tell the true Orient lover by his garbage tolerance level. I didn't mind it so much.

I observed about the garbage that it is much less noticeable when there are people moving over it, or squatting on it. In midafternoon, when everybody who can be is indoors, or late at night just before the curfew, you are more aware of the garbage than at other times of the day when the streets are crowded. I suppose this is because when it is crowded you are so busy watching the people and wondering how they can stand it. This is especially true at noon, when the street vendors squatting by their charcoal braziers offer for sale what everybody in Saigon calls "Chinese soup" and the customary stir-fried Oriental tidbits, everyone eating lustily and adding his dregs to the general slick of the overflow.

Sandbags

We had used them in my war. My personal experience with them had been mostly in Honolulu, right after Pearl Harbor, when we built or reinforced beach positions in and around Waikiki. But nowhere that I knew them did they ever reach the civilized, well-groomed aspect that they had in Vietnam.

Almost always they were green-colored. This made them match in color the interlocking, built-up metal members also in use for fragmentation and direct-fire protection. Thus adding a certain esthetic value. Sometimes the sandbags went up a full two stories. What was amazing about them was the way they kept their shape and their form at such heights. Later I got a closer look at them, and asked about them. A technique had been developed for spraying them with oil, and some composition. This hardened and made them as solid as any masonry, once they were placed. It accounted for their trim shipshape appearance, neat and military, squared off in their even lines and mounting pyramidal corners. They were everywhere in Vietnam. And only at the far-flung Border Ranger outposts I visited later, which were cut off and unreachable for resupply except by air, were there ever sandbags in disrepair, rotting and spilling and unshapely.

It was a consolation to know that, whatever else happened, we could always claim truthfully we had taught the South Viets how to take care of their sandbags.

Interpreters

An interpreter should be chosen with the same thoughtful care and judicious reflection you would use in choosing a wife, or a lover. He is about as intimate.

Unfortunately, most wives—and most lovers—are not chosen that way. And neither are interpreters. Time pressure and other pressures don't allow it. You wait and wait, and look and look, and then, when time is running out, or being without is just too painful to continue, you hastily choose from the best that is momentarily available at hand. Afterward, vain pride and a kind of primitive animal emotional loyalty require you to believe yours was an inevitable choice, made in heaven, and the best possible you ever could have chosen.

I must have interviewed a dozen interpreters. None of them had all of the qualities I needed, or thought I needed. Some of them didn't have any. There were mandarin-like professors of English who looked like they had never slept in a tent in their lives. There were ex-ARVN sergeants so tough they looked like they'd never slept anywhere else.

The two best interpreters I met were already employed by the *New York Times* bureau. Unfortunately for the *Times Magazine,* and me, all their time was already spoken for. Weeks and weeks ahead. By one feature writer or another. That was another way interpreters were like wives or lovers, or husbands. No matter how dissatisfied you were, you never turned loose of the one you had until you were absolutely sure you had a better one lined up. When I arrived, Henry Kamm who had arrived a month before me was off up around Hue with one of them. And when Kamm returned, another writer took off for Phnom Penh or someplace with the other one.

The one I finally married was turned onto me by

Henry Kamm. Kamm came back from Hue—with a clutch of successful stories, and took pity on me moping around the office in befuddlement, and looked up somebody who knew this man. I shall call him Vo. Vo had done some interpreting, but would only speak French to me. Although his English was at least as good as my French. But he had been a combat soldier, a captain, and did not look as if he would panic easily, like some of the professors I talked to who spoke a better academic English. And he was not a bloodthirsty wild-ass cowboy like some of the younger ex-soldiers I interviewed, who spoke a better GI English. Also, he came from around Hue, and knew his way around up there. And it looked like that was where I was going to go first. Whether I liked it or not. I didn't like it. Especially since Vo's and my reservations on the Hue plane were for seven days hence.

MACV

It is hard for me to describe the *Times* Saigon bureau. I may try later, but it was hard for me to know what was going on there, since everybody was so close-mouthed.

In any case, it had been a US Army car sent by Fred Weyand that had picked me up at the airport and delivered me to the hotel, and this information created quite a stir at the *Times* office when—somehow or other—it got known there. Also there had been a lot of phone calls for me, from the MACV public relations officer, before arrival. These continued after my arrival, never quite catching me, and they seemed to both excite and perturb the bureau chief, a small energetic sad-faced man named Sylvan Fox. "You sure seem to know a lot of people at MACV," he said to me several times.

It was Charlie Mohr, a tall, heavy, slow-spoken, bald and dome-headed newsman on loan to Saigon from the Kenya bureau, who told me to call General Weyand. Mohr was an old Vietnam hand. He had been there off and on, mostly on, since the first American involvement, was "in-country" all through Tet of '68, and had now been called back for the American windup. He never seemed to do anything except hang around the office, and occasionally advise Sylvan Fox, who seemed to defer to him. Otherwise he just sat around the office and read. He read omnivorously and with total concentration. News magazines, novels, girlie magazines, government papers, the subject didn't matter. Occasionally he would sit down and beat out some obscure story about the effect of Communist logistics in the U-Minh Forest in the southwest Delta or the religious influence of the Cao-Dai on infiltration in Tay Ninh, and send it in. He was an ardent gun nut, as I had once been, and passionately interested in every aspect of war. When I told him over dinner one night about General Weyand, Mohr said immediately I should call him. The Army had been getting tough about helping newsmen lately,— Mohr thought because of bad publicity they'd been getting in the press. Mohr didn't blame the Army, but said it made it hard for newsmen to do their job. But if I knew General Weyand personally, I should try to get him to help me get to Pleiku.

The first thing Weyand wanted to know on the phone was why I hadn't called him, then he invited me to lunch. Another Army car came for me. This seemed to cause some surprise and disjointed noses around the *Times*. The young colonel who came to pick me up fielded questions from the *Times* men about Weyand affably and politely and with total non-commitment. Outside in the car he smiled and said, "We've had to be a little circumspect with them lately, and they don't like it."

The MACV compound took up quite a bit of space inside the Tan Son Nhut gate, and looked about like any Army installation. No matter how you dolled them up, you could not hide their basically utilitarian nature. Here was the famous Pentagon East, the newsmen called it, head and center of everything the US Army did in Vietnam. And Fred Weyand, since the rotation home of General Abrams, was its commander. We walked down a lot of corridors, our heel raps echoing ahead of us.

In his office, Weyand looked worn and a little tired. He seemed genuinely glad to see me. As if anybody from outside was a thrill. He complained about exercise and putting on weight. He looked a little bit as if his mantle hung a little heavy on him. He said he would be glad to get everyone out of here and finish it.

He was an enormously tall man, Weyand, six foot four or five, with hands and feet to match, something awkwardly Lincolnesque about him, a Californian and a drawler. I had never heard anybody, neither his subordinates nor the Saigon newsmen, say a word against him, as they did about some others; that in itself was rare. His sense of strategy and tactics have been given credit for saving Saigon and Bien Hoa in the Tet Offensive of 1968.

After we talked a while, I told him my problem. He thought a minute, his face sobering. Then he drawled that he allowed as how there might be somebody going up to Pleiku in a day or so, there was this brigadier general named Healy who belonged up there, but was down in Saigon getting his teeth fixed, maybe I could hitch a ride up with him. I ought to like Mike Healy. He was sure one hell of a fighter, Healy. Weyand shook his head and smiled. Later Healy called in and I listened to Weyand telling him about me. They sounded for all the world like two college boys delightedly preparing to sneak a friend into a football game.

Over lunch in his quarters, which were comfortable but not elaborate, well protected, and not far from his office, I decided to tell him about my other projects. Observing a truce violation firsthand. Going out with an ICCS team. Visiting a North Viet or VC village. Weyand's face got suddenly authoritative. "Well, I'd like to help you. But we wouldn't want you to go around getting your rear end shot off. I wouldn't want to be responsible for that." Observing a violation was next to impossible, since there was no way of knowing where one would happen. Going out with an ICCS team might be dangerous, but would be vetoed by the Hungarians or Poles in any case. Crossing the lines would be *very* dangerous, and would get my visa revoked immediately. As for Pleiku, he was getting me up there but he couldn't guarantee I would get into Kontum, which was still cut off. That would have to be up to Healy. But he Weyand was giving explicit orders I was not to be taken anywhere where

41

I might get hurt. I just nodded. It was useless to argue with him. Nor did I feel very much like arguing. I felt Weyand was being overcautious in his restrictions, but I was in no position to argue.

Over coffee, Weyand suddenly grinned and as if he had been thinking it a while, said, "Gloria would be pretty mad at me if I let you get killed and 'wasted' her source of income." After a moment he shook his head and smiled. "I don't understand the *Times* sending a guy like you who is not anti-Army out here." I explained that it was the *Times Magazine*, and not the *Times*. But Weyand shook his head again and said it was still the *Times*. He went on to say he bet the fellows at the Saigon bureau were pretty mad at him. And went on to explain that lately he had clamped down on the news media pretty hard. He was used to being their whipping boy, and the Army was used to being everybody's villain over Vietnam, but he could not take a chance on their picking up something and twisting it and writing something sensational that might jeopardize the peace talks, and the POW issue. He had even had some trouble about helping to bring me out. Some people thought he was silly taking a chance like that. But he had told them exactly what he was telling me. "I think you're an honest man, and I think you'll write the truth. And that's all any of us want." I explained again that it wasn't my intention or my assignment to write anything political, but just a novelist's impressions. But if there was anything he thought might be detrimental to the peace talks or POW exchange, I'd be glad to clear it with him first. He just waved his hand. Nothing I wrote now would be out soon enough to have an effect. He just wanted me to write the truth I saw. He was more than willing to go along with that. Then he grinned. "Which, if I know you, you're damn well going to do anyway." He stood up, indicating lunch was over. Unfortunately, he had to get back to work. Healy would be in touch with me about Pleiku. The young colonel from the PR office would take me back to town.

Last Night in Saigon

It was noteworthy only for one thing. That was the fact that it was the first time I ever heard the words Dak Pek.

I had dinner with Charlie Mohr again, and afterward we adjourned to his room and Mohr got out his maps. He made no bones about how lucky I was to get into Pleiku right now. While I was there I should certainly go into Kontum while it was under siege. I said I wasn't at all sure Weyand would let me go into Kontum. Mohr shrugged this off and unfolded his map. I should also ask to go to some Montagnard area, perhaps at Ban Me Thuot. And I should certainly try to go to Dak Pek.

The names of course meant nothing to me. Mohr pointed them out on the map. Ban Me Thuot was a large town almost a hundred miles south of Pleiku, and an important Montagnard market center for the Rhadé tribe, which was the most intelligent and resourceful of the Montagnard tribes. Easy enough to get to. Dak Pek was the biggest, oldest and most important of the isolated Border Ranger outposts in MR

II. The only way to get to it was to fly in with a resupply mission by helicopter.

Dak Pek. On Mohr's map it was marked with a tiny penciled circle. Way up in the farthermost northwest corner of II Corps—MR II—astride Route 14, it was seven or eight miles from the Laotian border, ten miles from the boundary between II Corps and I Corps, seventy-five miles north of Pleiku. Formerly a hamlet, it had been made into one of the early US Special Forces camps, because of its terrain features, and it had been holding out ever since. A yearly pattern had developed. About twice a year the North Viets tried to take it and failed. It was built on five or six hills, and the NVA could take three of the hills but never the others. When the US troops had started their pull-out it had been turned over to the South Viet red-beret Border Rangers. The 1972 offensive could not take it either. At the moment, it was fifty miles inside the Communist lines as they were presently drawn just north of Kontum. I did not think Weyand or anybody else would ever let me get up there. But what a coup it would be for me if I could.

On the other hand, why did the idea of going there excite me so?

The Plei Me camp was another Ranger outpost I ought to get to, Mohr was saying and showed it to me, twenty-five miles south and west of Pleiku on his map. Then he put away his maps and began to tell me a story about the last time he had gone into Plei Me.

It was quite a story. And as he told it Mohr got more and more excited and enraptured. In 1965 the NVA had made a determined effort to reduce Plei Me, and

Mohr and another newsman had flown into it under fire. The newsmen had devilled the US Army commander until he let them draw straws to see who would go in. Mohr and another man had won. Mohr described to perfection the sense of mingled delight and regret at having won. The dry mouth, the flush of excitement just under the skin, the feeling of immense but reluctant determination. Going in, he had cursed himself for a moron, asked himself the old question—what the hell was he doing there? The only way to get in, with the volume of North Viet fire going up, was for the hotshot copter pilot to bring them in low and leapfrog over a little ridge, then feather his rotor blades and drop them straight down, jarring their teeth, their spines, and the soles of their feet. Then everybody dashed for a hole. Mohr's eyes snapped at me as he told it. The camp commander, an old friend Col Charlie Beckwith, met them grinning and shook hands, at the same time cursing them out for adding to his responsibilities.

I sat and studied Mohr. He was describing, highly intensified, the same feelings I got when I thought about going to Dak Pek.

We sat up a long time talking about what makes people like to do such things. We came to no valuable new conclusions. And afterward, I went back to my own room and stood looking out at the glaringly lit, deserted square below. For a quick moment I thought I saw my chittering toothsome apelike friend from Orly on the balcony outside, bouncing up and down and hooting and still following me. But when I looked carefully there was nothing.

Trip to Pleiku

An Army car came for me. Healy's plane was a U-21, a little five-seater, two-motor, propeller job. It made me think more than anything of the old Beechcraft Executive, a plane I had ridden in a lot, years before. It was apparently the executive workhorse of Vietnam. There wasn't much to see through the small windows. We had an hour and 50 minute ride ahead of us. I caught flashes of tough green mountains and once beyond those, of jungled draws and valleys and mile after mile of open red-earth country not unlike the central red-dirt plateau of Oahu. I had expected more jungle. Healy had the old soldier's trick I had forgotten about, of catching a half hour's nap whenever he could, and as soon as we were airborne shut his eyes. But after he woke, we talked.

Healy did not look like I'd expected. From hearing his voice on the phone with Weyand, I had expected a younger man, maybe thirty-five, blond and slim and burr-cut. Healy was forty-six, heavily muscled like a weightlifter, getting a little thick around the middle, with dark curly Irish hair that was not burr-cut. His broad face was pockmarked, he wore glasses, and every now and then one eye fiercely seemed to not quite track for a moment. Even at rest, asleep, he exuded a phenomenal fiery physical energy that seemed to be infinite.

Healy told me the fighting was easing off at Kon-

46

tum. The North Viets had tried mightily to take Kontum just before the cease-fire. As elsewhere, they had launched a major attack some thirty-six hours before the cutoff hour. When they failed, they had not stopped at the appointed hour. When they failed there, they had pulled back and sent troops around the city to the east, after the cease-fire, a week after the cease-fire, to cut Route 14 at a little pass between Kontum and Pleiku. That was what the month-long fighting had been over. If the NVA could show the ICCS they held Route 14 below Kontum, Kontum would theoretically lie within their territory and they could claim it. The ARVN had counterattacked this position on the road, and immediately been accused of violating the cease-fire by Hanoi. Now they were mopping up the area after the NVA had withdrawn. Not many NVA had withdrawn. They had wanted that road bad. And the ARVN had to push them back 2000 yards, in order to clear the road of fire from their big mortars. It had been a real fight, Healy said and grinned. The members of his advisory staff had dubbed the little Chu Pao pass the Rock Pile.

I had been told he was a "fighter," Healy, and not only by General Weyand. And I was too much of an old soldier not to appreciate him. And I was glad, whatever my intellectual propensities about war might be, that the United States still had men like him. He also had that kind of explosive wild-Irishman's charm, which could talk the pennies off the eyes of a dead nun, as they say. Back in the waiting room of the dispatcher's office at Tan Son Nhut— where he was sending his aide, Lt Charlie Vasquez, off to Bangkok for a week's R & R—he had stridden in in his bluff way and in seconds charmed and dominated everyone in the place. He was also a superb, masterful, old-fashioned Irish storyteller. The structure of his Second Regional Assistance Command (SRAC), I gathered, with himself as advisor to the II Corps commander, apparently ran right on down through the Viet chain of command to his junior-officer advisors at the regiment and battalion level. On the spur of the moment I asked him if while I was around there, he could get me into Kontum, and maybe as well have me flown up to the Border Ranger post at Dak Pek. His face sobered and got a little distant, and he gave me a funny little look. As if he thought I might be using him. He could probably get me into Kontum all right, for a short while, he said. But Dak Pek was out of the question. It was fifty miles inside the enemy lines, with antiaircraft positions all the way up.

It suddenly occurred to me—I thought I sensed—that Healy might not be feeling too happy about his assignment from General Weyand of squiring a novelist around. That I was getting off on the wrong foot with him. I didn't want that to happen. So when he asked me how long I'd been in service, I told him the truth. I'd been in five and a half years. But—I added—I was discharged early, in 1944. Invalided out. He looked up. Actually, I continued, with a vague intuitive flash of some irrational inspiration, I had wangled myself a discharge. After first coming back from the Pacific wounded, and then spending some time in a couple of Army jails. Perhaps he knew the type? Healy grinned suddenly, and nodded. I said I felt I'd used up all my luck and if I was sent to Europe I would never get back. Healy nodded again. Anyway, at the time I was in a lousy Quartermaster Gas Supply outfit with a bunch of other cripples. Otherwise, I said, if I hadn't wanted to be a writer, I'd probably have stayed in for the full trip. And suddenly I found myself launched into the telling of the long involved story of my reassignment from an Army hospital to Camp Campbell, Kentucky, which formed one of the main themes of the third Army novel I was working on. The point was, I had both loved and hated the Army.

Healy was an excellent listener. When I finished, he was silent for a long moment. Mine was certainly no tale of blind, Gung-Ho devotion. Then he rubbed his nose, and said the Army was only a tool after all, for molding and shaping your life into something. And then launched into a story of his own. Of when he had first enlisted and was serving as a private in Fort Riley, Kansas. He had been on guard duty on New Year's Eve, at the Officers' Club. And freezing half to death had climbed up on a wall and rubbed the frost off the window and watched the officers inside with their ladies and their dates, warm and drunk and enjoying their ball. When he got off post, he went back to his freezing barracks with its windowpanes knocked out and looked at the latrine with its stopped-up johns and pieces of turd frozen onto the floor and stormed downstairs and told the CQ to call the company commander and tell him to come over there. The CQ of course thought he'd gone crazy. But he insisted. And when the CC finally came, Healy took him upstairs and showed him the latrine, and the broken windows in the barracks room, where the heat was off. How did the Army expect men to serve in and believe in an outfit that forced them to live like that? he stormed. Like pigs. Like swine. The CC of course thought he was crazy, too—on New Year's Eve. The next day he was called up before the post commander. He expected at least a Special court-martial. Instead he was invited to go to Officers' Candidate School.

Telling me the tale, Healy was silent for a moment. Certainly, with his Irish talent, he told his tale at least twice as well as I'd told mine. I had listened captivated, thinking that after all perhaps I had struck the right note, hit the right chord.

That post commander had been a very intuitive man, Healy added. Certainly that night in Fort Riley had been one of the major turning points of his life. If they'd court-martialed him, he might easily have turned into a criminal. If they'd reprimanded him, he would certainly have quit the Army. He grinned his Irish grin. Instead, here he was. If I had had that kind of commanding officer, I might still be in the Army today. But then—he grinned impudently—the world might have lost a damn fine writer. We both lapsed into silence for a while.

Where was I staying in Pleiku? Healy asked after a while. I said I didn't know. I understood there was a hotel. Healy made a face. It was no good. If I wanted I could stay with him at SRAC. He had a guest room free for a couple of nights at least.

When the aircraft came down over Pleiku, it looked as if it had been a pretty town once, with lots of trees. Now it was an armed camp. Fortifications and artillery positions outlined it to the north and west. Convoys of troop trucks moved along all the roads in and out. Healy apologized for the pall of dust and smoke. It was the end of the dry season. He told me that in the '72 offensive the North Viets had gotten a quarter of

the way into the town, before they were thrown out.
We came in to land over a big lake which had a tall
statue of the Virgin on a pinnacle that ran out into it.

Pleiku

Healy was a fast mover. Over a fast lunch he learned
the situation had further eased around the Rock Pile,
during his two days in Saigon for dental work, but
that North Viet units were getting active down
around Ban Me Thuot. Also that VC teams were moving west of the road with rocket launchers, apparently to put fire on the highway. A young light colonel
with a pocked, scarred face as if he had been burned,
who was shipping home the next day, wanted to go to
Kontum to say good-by to his Viet counterpart. Healy
told him off to go later in Healy's personal chopper,
and to take me with him. Meantime, Healy's deputy
commander Col Charlie Black would take me on a
helicopter tour of the area, if I wanted, being always
careful not to go beyond the prescribed limits Healy
laid down. Then he left for his office.

The sense of leave-taking, of closing down, was
everywhere around the place. Every few days another contingent of officers and men of the Assistance
Command was being shipped out, to be flown to Clark
Field in the Philippines, and then home. The young
light colonel was only one.

I had never been in a helicopter. I guess I showed
it. My last advice on leaving Paris—from no less a

veteran than Jon Randall of the *Post*—was whatever I did, don't go riding around in Army helicopters. In any case Colonel Black grinned as we clambered up into Healy's command copter, and unobtrusively checked my seat belt for me. These belts had a lever-and-hook quick release that was hard to fit together if you weren't used to it. Then he handed me a set of earphones. The pistol-shot exhaust was deafening. In the air you had a tendency to lean far back in your seat. You had to take yourself in hand and force yourself, to lean forward and look straight down three thousand feet between your boots.

First we flew around over Pleiku, but lower now. It was still the same troop-packed, truck-gorged dust bowl. So many troops and so much matériel were a little awesome. Somebody somewhere had to control it. Then they rode me out and around the famous Mang Yang Pass on Route 19, thirty miles from Pleiku, the pass where *Groupement Mobile 100* had taken its final "waxing," then south as far as Healy would permit, then back west along the edge of what was now the VC (for VC read North Viet) -held territory. Over the intercom Charlie Black told me that the Frenchmen killed at the Mang Yang were buried standing up with their faces turned toward France. This did not move me much. It was a typical 19th-century-military thing the French would do. André Malraux would love it. Then step back and let us pull their colonial chestnuts for them again, all the while screaming Shame! at us for doing it. Along the way back on Route 14 we looked down on Montagnard villages, a number of abandoned firebases, a number of manned ones. Colonel Black kept up a running commentary on them. He had fought at most of them as a Special Forces soldier. It turned out he had fought at Plei Me during the same siege Charlie Mohr had just been telling me about. It was only about fifteen miles off to our west—he pointed for me—but was outside the prescribed limits General Healy had set.

At two places we flew over huge, lonely, abandoned US divisional main bases, all empty now, and largely dismantled by the Vietnamese, one for the 1st Cav and one of the 4th Division. These did move me. It was desolate country for a GI to live in for a year, set down in orderly city-like rows on the long flat strung-out plateau. All the blacktop road I saw, Colonel Black said on the intercom, including Route 14 stretching to invisibility in both directions, had been built and paid for by the US. Before us, the roads were all dirt.

In a few minutes we were almost back. I suffered a sudden depression. I was feeling more and more like some kind of a tourist. Which all too clearly was the way Black saw me, and was treating me. On a whim I turned to him and apologized for taking up his time. He simply smiled and shrugged, and said he was glad to get out of the office for an afternoon. Actually, he said, it was giving him a chance to see again a lot of old familiar places he hadn't thought he'd get to see before he himself shipped out. Back at Pleiku we picked up the young light colonel and headed out for Kontum.

The Rock Pile

Immediately, the whole operation felt different. Three thousand feet was the minimum we could fly, because of possible fire from VC (North Viet) groups still moving all around in the area. For Kontum, Healy sent a chase ship after us: another helicopter higher still, which if we got knocked down, or fell down, was supposed to come down and pick us up. Whenever I looked, he was up there behind us. US helicopters no longer carried machineguns. Colonel Black pointed out the Rock Pile area for me, a group of green hills in the dun terrain, through which the road wormed. A convoy of South Viet trucks at widely spaced intervals was moving on the road. They were moving rice, I was told by Black, Kontum had been short on rice for weeks. I looked away a moment, then looked back and saw one truck was now blazing merrily in the road. "You have a truck hit at three o'-clock," the young lt colonel's dry voice broke in authoritatively over the intercom. Almost immediately after, "You have a bomb strike at 4:30." I looked, and saw a thin funny haze in the air. Almost immediately smoke rolled up through it. I had never seen an air bombardment from the air. It was in the woods on our, west, side of the road. "You have an OB plane at two o'clock." I watched the observer plane swing west and circle back south. The bombers were not visible. The truck hit was by a small group with a B-40 rocket in the woods, still trying to interdict the road, Black said. They were probably shooting up at us right now, he grinned. Then we were past it all, and flew on, Kontum's river up ahead reflecting sunlight at us.

If Pleiku was an armed camp, Kontum was a town under siege. Fortifications and manned trenches with wire encircled it except to the southeast where the devastated airport lay. Several burned-out Russian tanks squatted sullenly in the devastation. We landed on a pad beside the Viet divisional commander's HQ. He was sorry they couldn't circle around for me, Black said, but it was a little too hairy. There appeared to be great personal affection between the young lt colonel and the even younger Viet general. They flung their arms around each other, when the general learned his advisor had come over to say good-by to him. He was fat and had a turned-up, wildly funny, humorous face, and had apparently been to the Army War College in the States, joked about the shell holes in his roof making fine ventilation, and grinned all the time while we had the inevitable cup of funky-tasting tea and talked. Things had eased off a lot since morning, he said. The two of them went off together. The ARVN general was one of the better ones of the young officers coming up, Charlie Black told me. "I'll borrow a jeep and run you around the town a little, but we won't have much time." Our chopper was too much of an open invitation.

From the jeep the town looked just like what it was: a one-horse frontier town. The business district was one long street of one-story, open-fronted buildings, two-thirds of them closed and shuttered now. Many people had left and become refugees. Anyway, there was little left to sell. Rice was rationed. In Pleiku most of the destruction of the '72 offensive had been repaired, but in Kontum there had not been the time. Along the main street armed troops strolled everywhere, with or without girls. In three of the little open-front billiard parlors one sees everywhere in Vietnam, Viet soldiers played billiards, their M-16 rifles leaning against the wall. At the far end of the street a new concrete sports arena had been blown half apart. Forms had been put up to start rebuilding, but the work had stopped there. Charlie Black was sorry he could not show me the bishop's residence, or the American hospital for the Montagnards, but there wasn't time. Back at the HQ the young lt colonel was waiting for us and we jogged out to the copter through the rubble to take off.

On the way back the young lt colonel thought it was safe enough now, after what he'd learned in Kontum, to fly over the road and go down and take a closer look at the Rock Pile. He wanted to see it one more time. He had spent a lot of hours down there, and had nearly lost his life twice. The place was one big damn slab of granite, under all that green. From the open door I looked down between my boots at a veritable moonscape. There did not appear to be much green left. In fact, the lt colonel was saying over the intercom, during the bomb strikes and artillery hits granite slivers had caused as many casualties as the shrapnel. Wreaked havoc among the North Viets. And also, of course, among his own South Viet people, when they finally got in there. At one point they were firing artillery point-blank at each other. All that almost a month after your cease-fire. From the other side of the helicopter he grinned at me crookedly across the mike. They had had to push the NVA back 1500 yards from there to clear the road to traffic. The NVA had broken contact, after that, and faded away. I looked down again, remembering terrains of my own. But none of them had been on granite. "See that little ridge there?" the young lt colonel pointed. "I spent a day and a half holed up behind that ridge. They couldn't get down to pick me up." The young colonel had a theory that every man had his breaking point, some sooner and some later, but everyone had one. He had not reached his down there, but he easily could have. Charlie Black looked unhappy and a little uncomfortable over this statement, but he did not say anything counter to it. When we arrived back at the Pleiku copter pad, I found Healy had invited me to dinner with his officers.

General's Mess

It had a little bit of the Rotary Club or Lions Club about it. But most of these men had just spent the last week voluntarily getting themselves shot at. A General's Mess is pretty much a one-man show. Everything centers around the general. The general officer himself is entrepreneur, stage manager, director, and performing star. As well as commander-in-chief. That can be very dull if the general officer is dull. Because the audience is captive. Healy ran his a little bit like an aggressive witty old-time Irish vaudeville performer. Not that anyone took liberties with him. But the laughter was genuine, not polite laughter. Healy was too good a raconteur not to see to that.

So here they were, assembled. Healy's field-grade officers, his junior-officer members of his staff, and the four or five other US officers who had been assigned to serve as ICCS members and wore the orange armband. Called on by Healy, these told wry anecdotes about their day's efforts to get along with the Poles and the Hungarians. Most of the men present had been hand-picked by Healy for his staff and a good many wore the Special Forces patch on the right shoulder as did Healy. I was aware that they were a tight, elite group of professionals. They had been left behind to do the dirty work of cleaning up. I was aware the discontented, the unhappys, and the inefficient had all gone home. But this group didn't smell like any defeated army to me. And they didn't seem to feel defeated. Most of them were good-naturedly aware that about half the nation considered them to be an anathema, and cheerfully accepted it. They were not unsophisticated.

There was a little bar in one corner. They began coming in promptly at seven, for one drink or two drinks, waiting until Healy sounded the call and led them to the U-shaped table. Healy had instituted a series of farewell dinners. This was because when they began to go they would go fast and in bunches with no time for farewells. So a long time back he'd begun what he called the "wine dinners." At which one officer would be lauded by Healy, receive a handmade Montagnard knife, and in turn make a farewell speech. The officer also was required to pay for the wine. The staff called these evenings "taking your turn in the barrel." It was all half joke, in Healy's style, but there was a ritual solemnity in it, too. And the Montagnard knives, in Healy's style also, were really worth having. Healy's adjutant had found, and nurtured along, a Montagnard knife-maker who made beautiful knives out of old jeep springs, using as his forge bellows an old bicycle wheel turned by hand by a small boy. Later I visited the village and watched him work.

The night I was there it was the turn of the Provost Marshall, and after a lot of jokes about cops Healy used the occasion to hold forth on an incident in which four young officers had gotten picked up drunk and one of them had slapped around an enlisted MP. Healy took a very jaundiced view of officers laying hands on enlisted men, and delivered himself of quite a lecture on officers' responsibilities. Apparently he and the Provost working together had managed to save the four, but been very severe in their own summary punishment. Sitting on the general's right in the "honored guest" spot, I knew my own turn was coming and when Healy introduced me, I tried to tell them a little of what I had felt about them looking at them earlier, without being too overt about an anathema. Then I sprang my surprise. I said I had a box of Cuban cigars with me, and I could not think of anything better to do with them than pass them out at the general's where we were all invited for a drink later—except possibly, of course, to smoke them myself. I think the gesture pleased Healy a lot. I know it pleased me to do it. The cigars were part of a carefully hoarded cache I'd brought from Paris, and which was shrinking alarmingly. But I couldn't *honestly* think of any place I'd rather put them. I had looked closely and I could not see one man amongst them who even looked like he might be involved in a military-industrial conspiracy to take over the United States.

Breaking Point

After an hour of drinking and a cigar most of the officers had left the general's rather spartan, pedestrian quarters. That was when the young lt colonel from the Kontum trip came over and sat down by me. He was a little unsteady on his feet and his eyes were bright. He had been relieved of duty as of five o'clock that afternoon. He wanted to know what I, as a writer and student of human nature, thought about his theory about breaking points. Was he right? Or wasn't he? What did I think? I said I didn't know. Probably I thought he was right. But I thought a lot of it depended on the individual. Not on just his psychological state, but on his physical nervous system. On his just sheer animal physical nervous system and just how much it could take, and for how long, and at what intensity. He nodded repeatedly as I talked. But I doubt if he heard me. He kept right on that he believed every man had his breaking point, and after that point, he got so he just didn't care any more. And when he got like that, he had reached it, passed it. He had not reached his, but he had come very close a couple of times. Up at Tan Canh last year, during the '72 offensive, when we had lost Tan Canh, he had almost reached it. Tan Canh was the worst he had ever seen, two weeks of it. For two weeks they had thrown everything they had available at Tan Canh. He shook his head. Then he began to tell me about Firebase November and his friend Bob Moore. Bob had lost his whole command at Firebase November, just last December. Only three months ago. A shell, or a big mortar, had made a direct hit on the command post bunker. When Bob came to, they were all dead except two. A division commander, two regimental commanders, the communications colonel, all dead. Except two, and they were just going out the door. When old Bob could walk, he went outside and found that *everybody* had gone. He was all alone there in the middle of the night. Not one man left. Two tanks were just pulling out of the perimeter and he ran over and managed to get a ride on the outside of one of them. And I was right up there over him, the lt colonel said, trying to talk him in. I couldn't go down in all that fire without giving the position away. He had tried every frequency on the console panel, to try and reach those tanks. He could see Bob but Bob couldn't see him and of course the radio at the firebase was gone. Anyway, nobody there. Nothing he could do. Finally he got them, but there still was nothing he could do. They got out finally, but Bob had passed his breaking point that night. He, the young lt colonel, had had letters from him since and they didn't sound like the same man. And *he* believed Bob reached his breaking point. Every man has one, and when he reaches it, he reaches it. He hadn't reached his but what bothered him was how was he going to know when he was going to reach it? Nobody could tell. But every man had his breaking point, he was sure of that.

"That's a lot of crap," Healy bawled heatedly from across the room. "Nobody has a breaking point unless they think they do. You can go on forever, if you have to." I beg to differ with you, General, Sir, the young lt colonel said; but I know different. "That's no way to think," Healy called heatedly. The young colonel said he didn't care, he knew what he knew. Later Healy helped him place a long-distance Army call on Healy's official phone to the colonel's wife in Washington, so she could fly out to San Francisco to meet him. After he came out of the bedroom, where the phone was, he drew himself up and saluted us all formally, a merry salute, smiling. Then he went off to bed.

"I'm glad he's going out," Healy said to me, heavily. "Of course, he's right, you know. Probably every man does have a breaking point. But I've never reached mine. Anyway, it's bad to talk about it. I don't believe in breaking points." A little later I went to bed myself, but I couldn't sleep. I couldn't get out of my head the picture of that young lt colonel drawing himself up, and saluting us merrily, standing at attention in Healy's bedroom door.

Night in Kontum

I had been told in Saigon by Franchini that if I did get into Kontum I should look up the bishop there. So I asked Healy for permission to go back the next day. Healy seemed to have taken a liking to me. I was glad, because I had taken a tremendous liking for him.

Anyway, Healy said he would fly me over himself and introduce me personally. Being Catholic, he knew the bishop. He's helped him out from time to time, with supplies and medical aid and such. He gave me an Irish wink.

Healy could not get away until midafternoon. When we got up, two big "hooks"—the big Chinook helicopters—were in the air, flying in huge bundles of supplies hanging under their bellies. Rice mostly, Healy said. The road was still not completely safe for trucks, as I knew.

Monsignor Seitz lived in a small villa tucked off to one side of the big imposing school he had started, and was noted for, out on the eastern edge of Kontum. Seitz was a famous character locally because he was the only white bishop left in Vietnam and refused to leave. He had been through the Tet Offensive of '68, and all through the '72 offensive. In '72 two of his village priests and seven of his nuns had been taken captive by the VC. He came striding in in a rusty cassock from where he had been gardening in his vegetable garden. It was late afternoon when the jeep let us off, and the sun was slanting in redly through the windows across the cool, shadowed tile floor as he came toward us in his sandals.

Healy went down on one knee and seized the bishop's hand and kissed his ring, with a kind of grand Irish theatricality. This seemed to embarrass the Monsignor. "Mais non, mon général, mais non," he protested. Having little experience of religious protocol I simply stuck out my hand. Seitz seemed glad to take it.

The bishop was a tall rawboned man, and spoke no English and was delighted when he learned I spoke

French. He seemed hungry to speak French to someone from the outside. On a table were snapshot photos, in cheap plastic holders, of four people. Three priests and a woman obviously a doctor. Two of the priests and the woman were white. In each press there was a photo taken while alive, and one of the same person laid out in death. As is usual, they did not look like the same people in the death photos. I asked about these and Seitz began to talk about them excitedly in French. Two of the village priests had been assassinated by the VC with pistol shots in the back of the head. The third priest and the lady doctor had stepped on land mines while out in the countryside performing their duties. They were Seitz's martyrs, and he seemed eager to have someone new to tell their stories to, and he talked on about them in French until Healy cleared his throat. He had to be getting back, Healy said; but if I wanted to stay the night it was fine with him, he would send someone for me in the morning. The bishop immediately chimed in with an invitation to stay, so I accepted.

When I went out with him to the jeep, Healy took me by the arm and drew me aside and said he did not expect anything to happen over here tonight. There shouldn't be any NVA attack, but there was always a possibility of one. If anything did happen he would leave instructions with the advisory command people to pick me up in a jeep and get me to a bunker. He couldn't do anything about getting me out during the night, but as soon as dawn came he would fly me out. I just nodded. But I felt distinctly peculiar. And somewhat pleased and excited.

In his study the bishop and I talked a long time. The Monsignor's face got set and grim, stubborn, when he spoke of the Communists. Seitz fully expected to die at the hands of the Viet Cong. If not this year, then next year, or the year after. He only hoped they would not be able to torture him, and make him say things he did not mean. He was sorry to see the Americans leave. They had been an enormous help, and always dependable, more than he had realized until he saw them leaving. The general was always helping him out with some little thing. The South Vietnamese just simply did not have that much themselves, to be able to help him. When I asked about the '72 offensive, he said neither of the priests who were captured was still here. One of the seven nuns was still in the local convent, and I could talk to her. Then he got up and went out and came back with a mimeographed booklet and gave it to me shyly. I must not look too closely at its literary style. Perhaps years ago in Paris he had a style, but no longer. In any case, his journal of the events from April to August of last year. When I got a chance to look at it, I found it terse and blunt like the Monsignor, eclectic in style, with little 19th-century Victorianisms and direct asides to the reader. Its contents made pretty grim reading. I still have it.

Seitz took me out and walked me around the grounds. They were pretty drab. They had not always been, but the offensive of last year had been fought right across his compound, when the VC came in from the east. The big beautiful school building, Western in structure but curiously Oriental in style, with its huge sloping tile roof, was partially demolished. But Seitz was rebuilding it slowly. You could see where the old tiles in the big roof stopped, and the lighter new tiles began. In the eastern end all the rafters had not yet been replaced.

Seitz went to have a room prepared for me, showed it to me and showed me how to work the oil lamp. The generator was cut off at nine. Then he drove me down to the convent to interview the nun. It was a largely unprofitable interview. The little Viet woman became easily confused and could not remember what she had said. It had been hard for her to march in the mountains. They hit her. They made her and another Sister wait on the priests, and then pointed them out to the villagers and laughed. They shouted and screamed at her. They beat everyone who did not want to be liberated. "They say one thing, and do another," she said in French, and shrugged. From there Seitz drove me over to the Patricia Smith American Montagnard Hospital.

Hilary

The Montagnard hospital was a shock, when you first saw it. When a Montagnard goes to the hospital, he brings the whole family. So there were families camped all over the dusty hospital yard, under the straggly trees. It looked worse than any small-town tenement. The Montagnards have their own standards, but they are not exactly what Westerners would call cleanly, or sanitary. They do not see much point to the constant washing of clothes. Of all the peoples of Southeast Asia the Montagnard tribes have suffered most in this war and have least deserved to. All of the Vietnamese, both North and South, look down on them with contempt. Their position is almost exactly analogous to that of our American Indian a hundred years ago. They are hardly considered human. A warm-eyed, kindly people, they continue to smile at everyone in a friendly way, though God knows why—or what friendliness they expect in return.

Seitz and I pushed our way through aisles crowded with healthy Montagnards talking to their relatives in the beds, until we found Hilary Smith (no relation to Pat Smith, the hospital's founder), a perky good-looking American girl with her hair in her eyes and sweat splotches under the arms of her grubby nurse's smock. She gave us a cheerful smile but said she had no time to talk now, they had just brought her in four casualties. Not combat casualties, but four Montagnard boys of twelve, who had found an unexploded B-40 rocket, and of course had had to throw it down on its nose on a rock, all of them getting wounded. One was serious, a chunk having gone into his side near his liver. Bad internal bleeding. Transfusions. I looked at the boy, who lay looking up with that look in his eyes of not knowing whether he was going to die. Hilary ruffled his hair. "Damn fool," she chided him, smiling. The bishop suggested she invite me to dinner, saying I probably had had enough of him. She agreed to have me, then showed me the three wards and the hospital kitchen. The kitchen was a hovel, out behind the building, where two lard cans of rice with a rare flake of meat in the boil, were simmering over a charcoal fire while clouds of flies buzzed over them. The cook was a gently smiling Montagnard in a loin cloth. Hilary grinned at me impishly and said while some people in the States might be shocked by their kitchen, they would be amazed at how well they got along with it in Kontum.

The hospital staff's quarters were just on the other side of the bishop's school, and Bishop Seitz dropped me off there. I waited quite a long time for them in their quarters, and ate up a lot of the chupata bread the Viet woman was cooking in the kitchen for dinner. It was night now and outside there was an almost constant rumble of outgoing artillery fire, and the crackle of small-arms fire. Shadow-shooting, Healy called it. He had told me not to worry about it. The Viets were expensive to keep in ammo. Once two or three rounds of something coming in exploded off on the other side of town, an entirely different sound. There was a lot of rumbling coming from far off in the direction of the Rock Pile but I could not tell if it was aerial bombardment or artillery. When the staff came straggling in looking exhausted, I found there were three of them. That was all the staff there was, with Patricia Smith away in America raising funds. Hilary; a young surgeon from New Zealand named Edrick Baker; and a young American ex-serviceman with long hair known simply as "John," who had come back to Vietnam because of a Viet girlfriend. John did the handyman work, Hilary the nursing, Baker the surgery and doctoring. However, in practice, everybody did just about everything, except the actual surgery. They all seemed eager to make it plain the hospital was independent, and not Catholic-run. Baker was quite young and, when asked, said he had come up to Vietnam originally because it gave him the kind of experience and practice in surgery that he needed, but somehow Vietnam seemed to get into your blood. But he was scared to death of the North Viets, and was thinking of going back somewhere and getting out of Kontum. He began to tell tales about the VC cutting off a Montagnard's ears and making him eat them in front of his village, and then cutting off genitals and making them eat them. I said both sides usually told tales like that about each other in every war. He shrugged hurriedly, and hurriedly went back to his food, eating fast.

The dinner was mostly "Chinese" vegetables and rice. There was a little plate of meat. I tried to refuse the meat but was not allowed. Baker finished quickly, and left. He had to go back to operate on the boy who had been hurt by the rocket. They did not know yet whether he would be all right. John the handyman wandered off somewhere and went to bed. So Hilary and I sat at the big table next to the kitchen and talked.

We talked quite a long time. Hilary came from the East Coast somewhere. Massachusetts, I think. But she had lived in New York. She had not started out to be a nurse. She was not a Marilyn Monroe-type beauty, but she was a very attractive girl. She was like a lot of New York girls I knew, well read, up on things, knowledgeable about plays, conscious of American politics; we had struck a rapport of knowledgeability from the start that Baker or John or Seitz could not share. I was fascinated why she would wind up in Kontum, in a hospital for Montagnards.

Mainly, it was because she had been a liberal, she said. There were other reasons, she added with a wry smile. But that was the main one. A passionate doctrinaire liberal. She had believed that the VC were more-sinned-against-than-sinning. That the Americans were evil in Vietnam. That the South Viets were totally corrupt. That the industrial-military complex had America by the throat. And she had wanted to do something about it, instead of just sitting in bars and talking about it. So she had studied nursing, to come out here.

Now though, she said, beginning to unburden herself, she was not so sure. She was still quote intellectually unquote a liberal. But emotionally she was confused, ambivalent. She had seen too many things the Viet Cong had done. Edrick Baker could be a little bizarre about atrocity stories. But they had mortared the hospital. Deliberately. To make the Montagnards afraid of it. They had come in during the offensive and shot five people in their beds in the wards. Pat Smith had had to evacuate her first hospital, farther out, because of the destruction they had done. All to discredit the hospital. Hilary felt they did not care about persons, but about quote the people unquote.

There was a big rumble outside, and she stopped a moment, and cocked her head. Then grinned. "That's outgoing," she said. "You get so you can tell the incoming from the outgoing." But what were "the people," if they were not persons? The VC made her think of nothing else quite so much as the religious fanatics of the Middle Ages. Communism was perhaps more of a religion, than a politics. And now she no longer knew what to believe. Would she go back home now, I asked. Probably. It was terrible to see the Americans leave. They had been so helpful, they were so kind. That General Healy of mine, he was a real darling. He was always bringing something over, or flying some patient out for them. It was going to be awful with them gone. She had never thought she'd be saying that about the Americans. For the moment at least she would probably stay on, at least until Pat Smith could find someone to replace her. But she could not forget the civilian medical team of Germans they had killed in Hue in '68.

Hers was one of only two requests I had in Vietnam to make a direct appeal to readers. The other was from an American colonel I met later in the Delta. "Tell them we need money," Hilary said. "Give them the address." I promised her I would, here it is.

Kontum Hospital Fund
522 Maritime Building
911 Western Avenue
Seattle, Washington 98104

When I finally left her we shook hands warmly. And, I kissed her on the cheek. For luck.

I walked back through the dark. The bishop had thoughtfully given me a flashlight. Halfway back I stopped for a while in the garden and turned off the light. There was a continual big rumble and flash of gunfire, like summer lightning, and the sky was lit up by flares. Every minute or so a new one went up and burst. Off to the west a salvo of "incoming" exploded, and then another. The shadow-shooters. I wondered what they all meant to do with all the shooting and what they thought they were shooting at. Right in front of me was a hole in the compound wall Hilary had told me about. A month ago a just random VC rocket had landed there, injuring an Italian journalist walking home as I was doing. Back in my tiny room at the bishop's I crawled in under the mosquito bar. My hairy, simian friend, quiet now, perched on the iron-rod foot of the bed, his head cocked on one side quizzically. I lay looking out through the windows at the flashes of gunfire of the shadow-shooters, in the unearthly glow of the flares they kept sending up, and I wondered what in hell I thought I was doing there.

The next morning at breakfast in the hospital staff quarters I found out that the Montagnard boy was going to be all right. Edrick Baker had been able to stop the internal bleeding, and the fragment hadn't damaged any organs.

The bishop came in, having walked over to say good-by to me, before Healy's advisory command boys came in the jeep to pick me up.

Flags

In Kontum and Pleiku, as in Saigon, the South Viet yellow flags with their three horizontal red stripes were everywhere. Not only on poles in the air, but painted on each house and outhouse. Apparently great store is set on these flags by the government. Some day, of course, according to the Paris agreements, there would be lines drawn and territorial claims made. Then any flag would be proof of ownership. So now in all of South Vietnam, apparently, it is a law that you must show the flag. Perhaps the VC helped to start this, by coming in at night and putting up a VC flag over a hamlet or village. Always it draws fire, or an air strike. So the people leave. They are afraid of reprisals if they take the VC flag down, so they leave. When they come back to their bombed-out villages, the VC say to them, See what Saigon has done to you? Saigon apparently has countered this with the flag law, though it is difficult to see why, or just what good it does.

Lepers

No trip to Vietnam could be considered complete without a visit to a leprosarium. Especially in the Central Highlands, where they were scattered all around. You could take gruesome pictures to titillate your friends back home. I had to admit I had a morbid fascination with it.

My first day at lunch in the SRAC mess I had noticed a rather mousy-looking civilian couple sitting off at a table apart with one of the officers. When I asked, I learned they were the American missionary couple who ran the leprosarium outside of town. Healy had ordered his chaplains to invite them to lunch twice a month to see how they were making out.

When I made my request, it was discovered it was the first such request anyone in the SRAC command could remember. Healy sent his Protestant chaplain with me. But the Catholic chaplain, a young Boston father, came along too saying he had always meant to go out there, but never had.

It was fifteen minutes out of town, two rather ramshackle buildings on a windswept red-earth hillside, sparsely grassed and almost treeless, that made me think of certain parts of the upland "desert" country of Arizona and New Mexico. All the lepers here were Montagnards, and there were the inevitable "visiting" families who had pitched a couple of big combination hide-and-Army-tarpaulin tents off away from the buildings. The Annamite Vietnamese, the young missionary doctor told us, considered the disease such a stigma that a great many of those who contracted it became suicidal. The superstitious horror, he told us, was only partly historical. The rest was because the disease was so physically ugly, and the Vietnamese were such a physically vain people. As far as they were concerned, it was strictly a "Montagnard disease."

In the height of the Middle Ages there were 19,000 lazar houses in the Christian world. In France alone in 1226, when France enacted its lazar-house law, there were 2000. It is amazing that so ill-organized a society as medieval Europe could even cope with such a magnitude of houses. The reason was superstitious terror. Into them, along with the lepers, and anybody with thickened skin or ulcerated sores, were shoved and segregated the horrors and fears and superstitious terrors of evil that medieval man did not want to face. Segregation was the only way they had to cope with the disease, but the incarceration of the leper also became a primitive ritual of purification for a whole society. Let the leper pay. Let him carry the sins of all of us. Let him be our sacrifice to the scourge of God. Even the Church told him he was Graced, as they drug him off and locked him up. By the end of the Middle Ages leprosy had all but disappeared from Europe, but the sense of horror and superstitious awe and fear hung on, clinging to the disease and to the person of the leper. Nowadays, when medical science knows about the low level of communicability, and that total segregation is only rarely necessary, it still hung on. Almost none of his patients were under compulsory segregation, they came and went, the missionary doctor told us. Only cheapness and ease of treatment, he said apologetically, made it necessary for them to stay together in leprosariums.

The problem of course, as always, was money. With enough money for medications, travel, and personnel they could all be treated amiably in their homes and the disease stamped out.

The good doctor, not being used to guests, was nervous and edgy with us going out, but as he loosened up he became quite informative. One of the biggest problems he had run into was a kind of self-hate that came as the disease progressed and which could not be eradicated. It was as if they despised their bodies for letting them down. There was a tendency to punish the offending parts. With the loss of all tactile sense in an extremity they were inclined to abuse it, let the hand burn itself, let the foot stamp down on sharp rocks. Much of the severe and unsightly ulceration and hideous autoamputation that were so associated with the disease was a result of this. A deep bruising that was repeated over and over and never allowed to heal. He showed us a few examples of these after we arrived. As he took us through the two wings that comprised his wards, he apologized profusely for having men and women in the same wards.

In the ward, I noticed the Protestant chaplain had begun to sweat a bit. After one ward he went back to the car and stood with the driver.

Shoes were a big problem, the missionary doctor said. The Montagnards were used to going barefoot anyway, and they damaged their feet. The expense of having a cobbler make sandals for so many mis-shapen and deformed feet was too great. He had gotten some of this new plastic that could be molded to the foot in warm water, and was encouraging the patients to make their own sandals. I looked at some of the pitiful examples, when he showed me his un-derequipped lab. Of course, it was pretty hard for them to do with fingers that couldn't feel well, he explained. It was the American therapeutic self-help concept. Where you teach an armless casualty to weave baskets with his toes. The doctor admitted it wasn't working too well here.

There was a group of women at an outbuilding soaking their feet in a medicated solution. One of them was a Montagnard girl who had just lost one of her big toes, and the doctor wanted to have a look at her and asked me if I wanted to walk over with him. I nodded. The Catholic chaplain declined, but I felt it would be impolite, and somehow deeply improper, for me not to go. The stub where the toe had been had a little pink tongue of flesh sticking out of the ring of dark thickened skin. It hadn't yet healed over. In Montagnard the doctor told her she was doing fine with her treatment and to go ahead and patted her on the shoulder. It was hard to get them to understand the treatment was what cured them, he explained. The girl kept smiling at us with embarrassment. Then she said something to the doctor and giggled.

She had said to tell me that she thought I was pretty, he explained, blushing. "Well, tell her I think she's pretty, too," I said. He did, and she giggled again. "I've got to go and wash my hands," the missionary said apologetically as he got up. "The contagion level is very low, you know. But after I touch somebody I generally wash my hands." Prolonged skin contact was the most common means of transmission.

Back in the car I looked down and discovered I had my camera still clutched in my fist. I had taken no pictures. Just after arriving I had walked through the breezeway between the wings out onto the back porch of the place and surprised two women sunning themselves. Seeing me, they had scampered back into the ward. One woman had only half of one foot and no fingers on either hand. The other woman had no feet at all and had crawled to the door on her knees, the characteristic doughnut-like scars on the ends of her ankles sticking up in the air. It had thoroughly inhibited my picture taking. But in the car the doctor told me I should have gone ahead. Actually, it would have pleased them to have their picture taken. The reason the women ran, he said, was because I had surprised them, and they weren't supposed to be out there at that hour of the day. But they wouldn't have minded a picture, nor would the girl. Only if there were three. The really backwoods Montagnards believed that three people in a picture brought ill to all three. Not two, or four. Only three.

Back at the SRAC compound I headed for my room, passionately intent on taking a shower, and feeling generally depressed. As I passed, General Healy stepped out of his apartment and fixed me with a shrewd eye. Well, had I had a good day? I said I guessed I had. Yeah, well, some things were pretty rough, Healy said astutely. And there wasn't any sensible way to explain them, was there? He invited me in for a drink.

Healy

There was always one thing with Healy. You knew his aggressive physical courage was monumental, and that his nerves were absolute steel. But with Healy there was an added quality of unstated sadness, an overblanket of sorrow, about things. Many men who don't have absolute physical courage have a deep irrational almost animal envy of men who do, and like to think of them as brutes. That is their defense. Other men look at them with boyish hero worship. But to a good professional soldier physical courage is like physical fitness, it is not a fetish but a foregone conclusion of the line of work, an accepted fact, a necessary tool of their trade, and they don't think about it much. But with Healy there was this additional quality of sorrow about life that was very appealing. Maybe his aging had something to do with it. Maybe it was just Irish. But you felt he had been born knowing that nothing could last forever. And he was quite willing to tell you that, if you asked him. But not unless you did.

Special Forces Soldier

Mike Healy was something of a legend, I learned. He wore a third dog tag that was famous in the Army. At someone's instigation he had shown it to me the night before. Hanging from his neck chain with the other two was a third identical plaque which, in the same GI stamped-in letters, said: IF YOU ARE RECOVERING MY BODY, FUCK YOU. It became so famous that once a visiting senator in Vietnam asked Healy to see it. Unembarrassed, Healy whipped it out and showed it to him.

A lieutenant, then a captain, of Rangers in Korea, Healy had gone into the Special Forces almost from the start. He seemed made for them. Wounded in the abdomen in Korea, he survived only because of the helicopter ferry service shown so graphically in the movie *Mash*. In Special Forces he went to Vietnam early, and was the model for one of the fictional characters in Robin Moore's *The Green Berets*. Later as a lieutenant colonel he was sent out to Vietnam again to replace Colonel Rheault as commander of the Special Forces, after the big scandal in the press about the killing of the double agent, when Special Forces was at its lowest ebb of public image. This time, he had accepted to come back again, as a brigadier, to command the II Corps advisory command for General Weyand, during the phase-out. When he went home at the end of March, he would go to command

79

the old 5th and 7th Special Forces Group at the John
F. Kennedy Center in Fort Bragg.

Since Healy was an old dyed-in-the-wool hard-core
Special Forces man to the bitter end, this pleased
Healy more than anything. Although the beret was
banned for wear now anywhere in Vietnam, with the
American combat units gone, Healy's personal green
beret reposed on top the wall cupboard behind his
desk in his bedroom along with his two baseball-type
field caps and his overseas cap. More than anything
the North Viets wanted to get the Special Forces out
of Vietnam, Healy grinned. "Nobody points it out
now, but Special Forces learned a lot of their dirty
tricks and tactics from the VC and NVA. They actually taught us how to fight a dirty war." Most of his
staff, chosen by him for this current assignment, had
served with him in Special Forces. One of his idiosyncrasies was his old sergeant major, whom he took
with him on every job, and who had served with him
in the field in Special Forces. When the sergeant major, a tough wise old bird of 42 as strong as an ox, came
over for a drink and to gossip—which was almost
every night—he and Healy would get out the tape of
Barry Sadler's *The Ballad of the Green Berets* and
play it. Sadler, a fairly famous country music record-
ing artist, had served in Special Forces under Healy,
and had written other Vietnam War songs. *Letter
from Vietnam, Saigon, Badge of Courage, Salute to
the Nurses, Ba-Mi-Ba* (the name of an excellent Vietnamese beer), *Garri-Trooper, Trooper's Lament*.
Healy had them all, and he and the sergeant major
played them all. This caused some looks to pass between some of the other non-Special Forces officers
having a drink in his quarters. But they were careful

that Healy did not see them. And in fact, I suspected that half the time Healy did it just to ragass them.

With March 28th coming up so fast and so little to do now that the Kontum road was open, Healy was edgy and had difficulty sleeping. So most of the nights I was there I sat up late talking with him after everyone else had gone to bed. He felt he was going to have a hard time adjusting to the quiet, regularized life back home. Like most of the former enlisted soldiers who had become higher-ranking officers, he had picked up a BA degree somewhere, I think the U of Colorado, by studying at night while stationed nearby. This was apparently a government policy, and lots of the non-West Point officers I met later had picked up BAs and even MAs during their tours of duty across the United States. I had mentioned one night that I thought Orientals felt very differently about an individual human life than we did in the West—as long, of course, as it was not their own life—but that my wife got furious at me for saying so and called me a fascist. Healy picked up on this and said he agreed, and said he felt the Orientals had a "wheel" religious philosophy about life while we in the West had a "ruler" religious philosophy. With the Oriental everything came back around, and then came back around again, and again. In our Christian thinking a life had a beginning point, and progressed toward a final end, and that was it. Naturally that would make us view an individual life differently, give it more value. The "wheel" versus the "ruler." He said he did not think the two could ever really get together and discuss anything in any way that made any sense because the terms of reference were so different.

We talked about the "New Army." And Healy stated

the concept which I would hear later over and over from "New Army" officers: having a strong discipline was no longer enough, you had to explain to these youngsters why and for what you wanted them to do something, you had to make them see why they needed to go out there and take a chance with their lives. Healy felt very strongly about this, having been an EM in the old Army. It was a far cry from the old Army I had known before World War II, and even in the middle of World War II.

The last night I was there a big-shot Medical Corps officer from Saigon, a colonel, was Healy's guest at dinner, having come up to check the closing down of the Army hospital in Pleiku. After that, there would be only a dispensary, which Healy's own medical officer would run. In the general's quarters afterward, the talk got around to why men did stay in the Army. The MC colonel, a huge dark very broad-shouldered Texan, said there wasn't any question about it with him. He loved the life. He liked the pay, and the travel, and the excitement, and the companionship. It was fun. Of course, he added quickly, he wasn't any infantry officer. He had been called up for a year, and he liked it so much when he got out he had gone back home and sold his practice and come back in permanently. "Are you divorced?" I asked. The colonel made a face. Yes, he was. Matter of fact, it was that first year of service that had broken up his marriage. Here Healy chimed in and said it was hard on soldiers' wives, being the wives of soldiers. And it got harder to take assignments overseas, as the years went by. I had never heard him talk much about his family.

Later that night after everybody had left Healy and I sat on, and he talked about his family. It had been very hard on his wife, all the time he spent away. Naturally she didn't like it, and she liked it less and less as the years ran on. He felt he hadn't spent enough time with his kids. He had six sons. In one way, he felt he hardly knew them. This would probably be his last tour overseas, he figured. But the kids were all so grown up now it didn't matter. It was the bane of a soldier's life, this being away. Two of his boys had flubbed up pretty good. One of them had botched up his career at West Point and let himself get dropped, and was just drifting. Another was a longhair and wanted to be a writer. He grinned at me and said, "Maybe I'll send him to you in Paris." I said I'd love to have him. Mind you, he was no hippie dropout, and he was probably the most intelligent of the six. I said I had lots of friends' kids coming over from time to time, wanting to be writers, but none of them ever wanted to work hard enough. That was it, Healy said. This whole generation didn't want to work for anything. Anyway, this was probably his last tour overseas, he said again and bounced a big fist on a hard thigh. He hated to leave Vietnam. Quite a lot of his life had been spent here, with these people. Then he said something I would hear over and over again the rest of the time I spent in Vietnam. In about five years he wanted to come back, Healy said, and see how things were still developing. Even if it meant using his own leave time to do it. He stood up and blew out his lips in a sigh. It must just be that he was getting old. He said he'd walk outside with me.

Dak Pek Again

As we stood breathing the night air, Healy without being asked suddenly said he had been thinking about my Dak Pek request. He had looked into it and he thought there was a way he might be able to swing it.

I suddenly felt excitement rolling all over me just under my skin, like a flush.

It was entirely possible, Healy said, to tack a copter onto a Viet resupply mission to Dak Pek. They went up every week or two. But that would pose certain technical difficulties. Translation was always a problem. And could cause a time lag in understanding orders that, in the air, could be downright dangerous. Also he did not trust the Viet copter jockeys as much as his own. If you went down in enemy country, it would be the Viets who had to come down and pick you up. They had been known not to come. Had I noticed how the US ships were no longer armed with machineguns? The Viet ships were still armed. But that only meant that they might shoot you by mistake, if they got nervous coming down.

So he had vetoed that method for the moment. But Charlie Black would dearly love to get back up to Dak Pek one more time before he shipped out. Black had helped build that base. So Healy was looking into the possibility of sending Black with me. In his—Healy's

—command copter, with another of our own ships flying chase.

This presented problems. Healy had to have permission, to make a mission so far into enemy country. And if General Weyand ever found out, he not only would absolutely forbid it, but would have Healy's and my ears in the process. General Weyand had given him explicit orders not to let me go anywhere dangerous. Because of Gloria. He never should have let me stay overnight in Kontum.

Healy grinned. Of course, if it was already a *fait accompli* there wasn't much General Weyand could do except give us both an ass-eating. Hands in his pockets, Healy leaned back in the night air, stretching his legs. Matter of fact, he would like to go himself. But he didn't see how he could make it.

Anyway, all this would take four or five days to arrange. Even a week. If it was possible to arrange at all. And he wasn't guaranteeing it. Meantime, there was a big Buddhist funeral over in Hue tomorrow, and maybe I would like to see that. The chief Buddhist monk of all Vietnam had died some time back and was being buried tomorrow. It would be quite a pageant. If I wanted, he would fly me over in his plane tomorrow morning.

I accepted immediately. Dak Pek was in the way of becoming an obsession with me. And I had about given it up. And, I intended to go to Hue eventually anyway.

I could nose around over there a few days, Healy said, until he found out about this Dak Pek thing. And if he could swing it, he would let me know and send his plane for me. I had an interpreter in Saigon, didn't

I? Yes, I said. But I didn't have any hope of getting him up to Hue that quickly.

No problem, Healy said. If I gave him his name early in the morning, he would call Saigon and have them locate him and ship him up on an Army plane tomorrow. They had planes flying to Phu Bai airbase at Hue every day.

It was late, and there were no other lights on in the fortified compound. The fortifications looked unused in a long time. Not since Tet of '68 probably. Healy turned to me and looked as if he were about to say something else. Instead, he grinned and stuck out his hand. After we shook, he went in his door, his broad back looking curiously lonely, in some way I could not exactly define.

I went to bed excited as hell over Dak Pek.

Funeral in Hue

I got away late the next morning. At Phu Bai airport a helicopter was waiting to fly me the ten miles into Hue, and my interpreter Vo was waiting for me on the ground.

I had stumbled onto something. Through a set of fortuitous circumstances, through knowing Fred We- yand in Paris, and then through becoming friends with Healy, I had fallen illegitimate heir to the Ar- my's transportation system. I didn't know what it had been like before. But after the cease-fire, the hardest thing for a reporter to do in Vietnam was to get himself transported from one place to another. I figured I'd be a fool not to utilize it.

I could hear all my New York liberal friends hooting. The same ones who, with one philosophical jerk, had so cavalierly pulled the rug of humanity from under the feet of the US Army. Jones has gotten himself brainwashed by the Army. Well, I figured I was no more brainwashed than Mary McCarthy had been by the North Vietnamese, when they invited her to Hanoi and squired her all around. Less, probably. I knew how shitty the Army could be.

From the air Hue looks reasonably pretty. Much of the destruction done in Tet of '68 has been repaired. Compared to the bare countryside of salt flats and ricefields outside it, it looks to be sufficiently green, with lots of trees.

On the ground it is dirty, dusty, unimaginably hot at the end of the dry season, and the trees that look pretty from the air are spaced too far apart to be much aid against the murderous sun.

The funeral of the chief Buddhist bonze of Hue was the big religious event of the year. Over 100,000 people had journeyed to the city for it. It was also a big political event. It was in the Imperial City of Hue that the Buddhists began the revolt against Diem in 1963 that ended in Diem's overthrow, and Hue was still a big Buddhist stronghold. President Thieu had flown up for it, and had even brought along his deposed premier, Nguyen Cao Ky. It was the first time Ky had appeared in public in months.

In the streets the crowds seemed to be composed mainly of soldiers, groups of the gray-clad young Buddhist bonzes, and the white-clad schoolgirls in their conical straw hats, black pants and long white overblouse of the *ao-dai*. The jeep I'd been loaned, under command of an ARVN captain, had to move slowly through the crowds and the pall of dust scuffed up by thousands of sandaled feet in the heat. By jockeying back and forth, and arguing his way past several groups of security police guarding concertinas of barbed wire stretched across the road, the ARVN captain was able to pull up close enough so that, standing on the jeep hood in the noon sun, we could see the funeral cortege.

It went on for over an hour. Miniature pagodas and shrines, painted in bright primary colors, borne on the shoulders of sweating bonzes. Upright silken banners of purples and blacks and golds. Companies of black-clad mandarins with their formalized black turbans. Hundreds of groups of Girl Scouts and Boy Scouts, in their uniforms. The uniforms were worn-looking, and the wide brims of the Scout hats, instead of being stiff, hung down over the boys' heads. But it was an impressive show, an impressive display of the Buddhist strength, and all around us children munched on cones of shaved ice covered with syrup and watched with big eyes, and adults whispered together quietly.

Afterward, in the crowded business district on the other bank of the river, the ARVN captain, my interpreter and I ate lunch in a pleasant little open-front Viet restaurant. We were its only customers. When I asked about this, my interpreter whose home village was just outside Hue said that the people were not eating in restaurants now, with the Americans leaving. Too many sources of income were drying up, and they were saving their money. Also, this restaurant had been heavily patronized by Americans and people were not sure they ought to be seen there, now. The owner, in fact, was thinking of closing it up and going somewhere else. "Here in Hue," the interpreter said, "where they are so much closer to the North, they are afraid. They remember 1968."

This was one of the reasons I had wanted all along to come to Hue. Everywhere I had been in Vietnam so far, people, people like Hilary Smith in Kontum and the *Times* office boy in Saigon, had mentioned Hue and the Hue massacres of the 1968 offensive.

Outside in the hot street, as we drove to the Imperial Citadel to inspect the massive damage done in the Tet Offensive of '68, the street vendors and temporary stalls put up for the celebration were doing a big business selling the "Chinese soup" and cones of syrup-covered ice.

Hue and the Viet Nation

I quickly took a dislike to Hue. Perhaps it was the massive heat. But Hue put me in a depression. After the Central Highlands, the heat of the coastal plain of Hue was like a blow, a constant weight, a palpable presence in the nostrils each time you breathed. It seemed to me this affected the thoughts of the people.

Everybody talked about Hue as the symbol of the grace and beauty of Viet culture. I found it ugly and pretentious. If the city was to symbolize the grace of Viet culture, then it must also be willing to serve as a symbol of the other side of Viet history; the arrogant, the cruel, the willful, the bloody, the false-proud, the cantankerous, the conquest-seeking.

Hue was supposed to be the gentle, leisurely cultural capital of the ancient days. Was called the most beautiful city of Vietnam. A city of peace in a region of terror. The Buddhists liked to compare it to a lotus flower growing out of mud and slime. It was supposed to be inhabited by a sophisticated independent people who remained aloof from both the corruption of Saigon and the Big Brother oppression of Hanoi. I found it none of these things.

Perhaps Tet of '68 had changed it in some basic way. But it could equally be called a city of blood and terror. Tet had not been all that different from past histories. Hue's history of "Oriental cruelty" was as great as its history of "culture." Viet emperors and their Viet armies had fought each other over it, and in it, for hundreds of years, the winners consistently exterminating the losers, the families of the losers, and everyone who helped them. One losing emperor watched his father's bones dug up and urinated on by the soldiery. He then was torn apart alive by elephants. It had been a hotbed of political jockeying and in-fighting and intrigue since the Nguyen war lords made it the capital. I suspected as many people had lived in terror there as had lived in peace or beauty.

But Hue wanted it all one way. Vainly it wanted the grand reputation for beauty and culture without any of the bloody ugly stigmas. Wanted the distinction of exquisite sensitivity and to bury all the rest and pretend it had never existed. And I was beginning to suspect the Viet people wanted to have it the same way.

Hue's Massacres

Whatever else they accomplished, the Hue massacres and the Tet offensive effectively turned the bulk of the South Vietnamese against the Northern Communists for a long time to come. In South Vietnam wherever one went, from Can Tho in the Delta to Tay Ninh to Kontum in the north, and of course in Hue, the '68 Tet massacres were still being talked about in 1973.

In 24 days of February, 1968, the North Viets and VC systematically and deliberately shot to death, clubbed to death, or buried alive some 2800 inhabitants of Hue —government personnel, administrative personnel, students, teachers, priests, rural development personnel, policemen, foreign medical teams, local political leadership; anyone and everyone who had anything to do with training the young, running the city, or aiding the citizenry in any way.

There was no question that the killings were part of a planned campaign. Detailed written plans were distributed which divided the city into target areas, and named the principal human targets living on each street. The targets were to be arrested, moved out of the town, and killed. Attempts were to be made to gain the sympathy of the Buddhists and the French, but other foreign civilians, especially Americans, Germans, and Filipinos, were to be taken and "punished."

The North Viet and VC leaders apparently knew

they could not expect to hold Hue for very long. It is difficult to see what they expected to gain from the killings. What they gained was the undying enmity of just about every South Viet who might have been wavering toward accepting them.

It was only after the Tet offensive and particularly the Hue killings that the South Viet government was able to institute a general mobilization and draft, something it could never make stick before, thereby nearly doubling its military strength. Tet and Hue, ironically, left the South Viet government stronger than it had ever been.

The battle for Hue itself received enormous publicity in America in 1968, but the aftermath didn't. It was slow in coming to light, partly because the people were afraid to talk about it for quite a while, partly because it took a long time to find all the bodies, many of which had been marched—"on the hoof," so to speak—into the remote mountain passes before being killed. Some pieces were written about it in America but dropped from sight quickly. As the battle receded, so did the interest.

It was not until a year later that many of the mass graves were discovered. And it was not until November, 1969, when a controversial Nixon speech used Hue as a justification for slow withdrawal, that the subject got additional attention in the press. But at the time, few American reporters saw fit to take it on and go into it. Nobody tried to do a serious exposé. Hue was no longer news. Anti-US feeling was popular at home. Why buck it in the cause of unpopular truths? Much better to concentrate on our own horrors at My Lai. At least we could do something about that.

Several American writers, at least one of whom had

lived in Hue and visited it after, wrote apologias to minimize the massacres and tried to prove the killings were not North Viet-Vietcong policy, but the acts of angry soldiers in the heat of battle. Even though there were refutations of this work, the Hue killings somehow came to be thought of as a Nixon political ploy. They had not really happened, not as far as liberal America was concerned.

But the reasoning was specious: Applying our American western-film morality, we decided that if we were the bad guys, then the other side must be the good guys. And the good guys couldn't do something like Hue. We refused to believe it. The North Viets had handled the affair just about to perfection—but our answer did not necessarily follow. One of the last of the Hue graves to be found was a fresh bubbling mountain stream miles back in the mountain fastnesses. In its jungled bed were the bones of some 400 bodies, all washed and jumbled together by the pure, sweet water. Inspection of such separated skulls as were found (skulls, being round, washed away) showed that almost without exception the citizens had been clubbed to death, probably with rifle butts or wooden bars. It is not known whether this was done to save 400 cartridges, or as a gesture of contempt. Tumbled all together as the bones were, almost none of the bodies were identifiable. All were buried together in one large mass grave.

This was certainly not the result of the "heat of battle." When one sits and contemplates what it must have been like to be on such a march, the thing is kind of breath-taking. Civilian men and women, out of training physically, unused to heavy marches, arms tied behind them, mile after mile and hour after hour, climbing steep rocky mountain trails in that heat, and descending them which is even more fatiguing, knowing almost certainly what the end must be. It is no easy thing to club down 400 people. It couldn't be done simultaneously, not without a guard for every prisoner. So they probably had to take them by bunches. But bunches of how many? One wonders what it must have been like to be a guard, on such a trip. So far as is known, no VC soldier or North Viet vet has come forward with a formal protest to his government about the atrocity, or made a film about what it felt like. So far as is known, neither the VC's Provisional Revolutionary Government, nor the North Viets' Democratic Republic of North Vietnam, has made a formal investigation of it, or sentenced any of the participants.

Monastery

In spite of the heat the drive was beautiful. The Thien An Benedictine monastery was located about five miles southwest of Hue. Outside the city, and onto the unpaved back roads, the tropical and semitropical vegetation became profuse. Tall stands of hardwoods and stands of tall pines covered the hills, the sun raying down through and dappling the ground. Clusters of thatched houses clung together in tiny hamlets every couple of hundred yards, buried in broad-leaved banana plants providing both shade and nourishment. The silence was immense.

Large-eyed children peered out at us. Twice we passed groupings of squat bottle-shaped Buddhist wats, small ones, ancient-looking and black with age. The monastery on its hill overlooking a lengthening valley came into view around a curve of the road. It didn't look damaged. The North Viets had occupied it for several days during the '72 offensive. Then we came around the foot of the hill and up a rise to the courtyard, and saw that the back of the building had been just about disemboweled. Pieces of rafter hung out over the empty space where walls should have been. An arched stone doorway rested askew on its piers.

It was the American artillery, the Vietnamese abbot told me. I must have looked embarrassed, because he smiled. That was the war, he said gently. The Americans destroyed the buildings, the Communists killed the people. He showed me the library, which was one of the big rooms with its exterior wall gone. One diminutive Viet monk with his skirts hiked up was busily sawing a large, tough beam that would go into the wall. It was sorrowful, the abbot commented. They had lost so many volumes. Old, irreplaceable ones. Also it took so long to do repairs. They had so few people now. When he found out I was interested in Tet of '68, he went somewhere and brought back an old dusty shoebox.

He was a squat, slender man, much younger than I was, with that long waist and bandy legs Vietnamese tend to, and the closely shorn at the sides, unruly on the top, haircut Oriental priests seem to affect. He had been here during Tet of 1968, though he was not the abbot then. He began to go into a long, accurate, detailed disquisition on the tactical methods and maneuvers of the Communists.

The shoebox contained a dusty pathetic collection of photo snapshots, signed affidavits, last letters of people who had been executed. There had been three elderly French fathers living at the monastery in 1968. Two had been taken and killed, the third was still here. I could talk to him if I liked, but his mind had been affected by the experience and he did not make much sense.

Local people had warned them that the VC were coming. During the fighting in the city there had been 2000 refugees living in and around the monastery. Perhaps that was what had brought them. The refugees and the fathers had split up into small groups and left by various back trails. A number of groups, including the one with the two French fathers, had been caught and captured. The procedure was to hold a People's Court in the nearest hamlet, at which the crimes of the victims were read out. The victims were then taken outside the hamlet, made to dig their own graves, clubbed or shot, and the villagers were ordered to fill in the graves. They were not allowed to mark the graves. When the stories finally came out and the graves were uncovered, the two fathers were found buried in a group of fifteen. One of them had been buried alive. The villagers brought a tale to the monastery that one of the elderly fathers had defied the Viet Cong, called their People's Court an abomination against God, and refused to accept its verdict. For this they buried him alive without clubbing or shooting him.

The abbot smiled and pushed a small snapshot toward me. This particular group had been buried in sand, probably because it was easier to dig, and was thus well preserved, and the position of the French father's body seemed to bear out the story.

We talked a long time in the high, cool hall. It gave off an unreal, incongruous tranquility, considering the nature of our talk. The abbot did not know why the North Viets had instituted the massacres. It did not make political sense. Personal revenge. Fanaticism. The South was guilty; it must be punished. The abbot once had believed in the war of national liberation. He had been on the side of the Viet Minh. Now he felt the war was no longer that. It was the political war of the Communists. Now, it was the war of the religions. When I stared at him, he explained that he considered Communism a religion. The religion of the Anti-Christ to be sure, but nonetheless a religion. In our age politics had become religion, he said.

I did not feel it was my place to tell him that in its day of power the Church had made religion politics. Anyway, that was four hundred years ago. I asked what he intended to do now. He said he intended to stay here. What if the VC came again? He did not think they would. They were too hated. But if they did, he would run away and hide again. Then he would come back.

He insisted on showing me around the rest of the establishment, describing at each point what it had been like before. Parts of it, the still untouched parts, were still very beautiful. At the curve in the road, I looked back up at it on its hill, brooding over its lengthening, pretty valley. From the front you could not see the destruction or the holes in the walls the American artillery had made.

Quang Tri Aerial

The North Viet prisoners were being turned over to the Communists at Quang Tri, north of Hue. Of course the North Viets insisted on maintaining the fiction that they were Viet Cong. Quang Tri was where the two lines face each other across the Thich Han river. The US colonel with whom I wangled a helicopter ride north was at the MACV HQ in Hue. He had been assigned to the four-power Joint Military Commission (JMC) and wore the orange armband with the big black 4 on it. The colonel was a man of about my own age, who had come out of World War II, and was worn and sardonic with wise eyes. He was, he said, X+36, which meant he had 24 days to go—X being the day of the final Paris signing. Then he would turn in his orange armband and leave Vietnam forever, and glad to go.

We took off from the MACV pad. Hue unrolled and fled beneath us, people and trees and houses curiously foreshortened from our aerial perspective. The sky was cloudless. Except for a few cotton cumulus which seemed to condense off the tops of the black mountains to the west until they broke free like bubbles from a soap pipe and swung eastward with the breeze.

The colonel was glad to have unjaded eyeballs with him. He had, he said, made this trip so many times he felt like a Rye commuter. He told his pilot to stay down low so I could see, and pointed out things for me. The young warrant officer pilot with his big droopy 1880s mustache took him at his word, and after grinning at us used the opportunity well to display his skill. I sat enthralled and watched treetops flash past me at eye level through the open doors, remembering again what Jon Randall had told me about Army helicopters in Paris.

About a mile outside of Hue it began. On both sides of the road, rusting burnt-out and abandoned trucks and jeeps and personnel carriers lined the ditches and spread out into the fields. Most of this stuff was South Viet, left behind during the retreat of 1972. The colonel grinned. I should have seen it six months ago before they started cleaning it up.

As we fled farther north, the abandoned matériel began to thicken, and Russian tanks, which my eye had learned to recognize in Kontum, began to appear in the ether debris. We flashed across a second river, which the colonel said was the My Chanh, whose bridge was down; another had been built beside it on wooden stilts. The battle debris and burnt-out vehicles began to thicken even more. The My Chanh was the line at which the South Viet Army had stopped the Northern thrust and begun to roll it back. As far as the eye could see in both directions out across the sand flats and fields, there was a carpet of busted trucks, tanks, APCs, jeeps, command vehicles, artillery carriages. Across the plain, ruined villages thrust up out of this oxidizing mass amongst the fragile green of their splintered trees. Six months ago you could have walked from here into Quang Tri without touching the ground, the colonel said with a smile.

There was a huge number of the dead tanks strung

out across the plain, and the colonel told me the enemy had made terrible mistakes in using their tanks. They had really flubbed it. They were a strange breed. They thought because they were great irregular light infantry, that made them great with tanks, too. They never should have used their tanks at all. They weren't tankers and they had committed them piecemeal, two or three at a time, so that they were never able to use either their mass or their firepower to any great effect. The classic mistake. The cost had been staggering. Well, I could see the cost. He had had his people put an individual bounty on tanks, and sent out individual volunteers with one-man rocket launchers. Once they got over their first fear, they had torn them up. Used their own tactics back on them. By "his people" he meant the South Viet division he was advising.

We flashed over four burned Russian T-54s sitting together, low enough to see the individual rivets, and the colonel pointed. He had had a personal hand in that set. He told the copter pilot to circle them. We did, round and around, so tightly I had difficulty keeping my eyes open against the chest-sucking vertigo. There had been six, the colonel said. But after they had hit the first four with launchers, the crews of the other two had abandoned and the two undamaged tanks had been run into Hue. He looked at them again a long moment, his eyes lighting, then told the pilot over the intercom to go on.

It was dumfounding, astounding, near unbelievable to sit there and see spread out before us so much wealth—so much *money*—in rusting and wrecked machinery.

Ahead, below us on the road were the trucks of the

prisoner convoy, the second convoy, the colonel said (there would be four runs today). The North Viet prisoners in their maroon prisoner uniforms stared up at us. Many of them wore white cloths tied over their heads in the trucks, the two ends hanging down the back of the neck. They looked very healthy. They were being flown up by C-147 and landed at Camp Evans outside Hue and then brought the rest of the way by truck. Then we were past them, flying carefully alongside the road. It was forbidden to fly over them. Past them, we crossed the road, and swung west to come in by the bridge. The colonel thought I ought to see the flags. It was against the rules, to fly alongside the river like this. God knew why. Some niggling point about us observing them. But he didn't think they would fire on us today, he smiled.

We were past the bridge almost before you could see it. Two enormous banners on tall poles, one VC, the other South Viet, snapped in the breeze and the sun, each set exactly at the water's edge on opposite sides of the river bridge. They didn't look brave. They looked ridiculous. Up there, trying to outdo each other. I looked at the colonel. He grinned, and nodded. "Somebody has said that Vietnam is the biggest fifth grade in the world," he said; "I believe it." Then we were over the city of Quang Tri, and the colonel's remark took on sinister implications.

It was sort of stunning. Mind-numbing. The first thing you noticed was the color. There wasn't any. It was like a black-and-white movie. Everything was gray. Covered with coat after coat of the dust. Dust from the enormous artillery barrages both sides had poured into it day after day, and from the US aerial bombardment. A good-sized town, but in the heart of the city not a single building was left standing. The streets themselves were obliterated. Even the thick walls of the old Citadel had been smashed down to their foundations. Here and there part of a wall or a bent girder or a spaghetti twist of steel reinforcing stuck up out of the rubble, becoming a landmark by its height.

For some reason known only to them, tactical or political, the North Vietnamese had made up their minds not to lose Quang Tri. They had poured incalculable numbers of men into it, only to be thrown out finally, rooted out house to house by the South Viet paras and Rangers. Maybe they wanted it to be some sort of symbol. The other side of the river would have made a much better holding line. Only in the remotest outskirts to the south were there any whole buildings recognizable as such, and these were ruined: roofless, gaping with holes, a corner support gone so the whole thing sagged, entire walls missing.

The volume of explosive fire at any given high moment must have been stupendous. Your time sense becomes totally deranged in a situation like that. The second hand of a watch seems to take eons to move from one mark to another. This had gone on for something like three weeks, the worst of it. I could not imagine any soldier wanting to stay in a place like that and fight for it. But both sides did. Stubborn fifth-graders. The South Vietnamese had won it, with our air support.

The whole place was full of mines and booby traps, the colonel told me as we circled down, so I should be careful where I walked.

Low Level

If you look straight down, everything is a blur. Out away from the ship stationary objects move past so fast you have to catch them with your eye up in front and move your head with them as they pass, to even get a cursory look at them. Trees come toward you. As the pilot swings the ship a hair to go between them. Then zip past in a total blur. The solid rows of trees, as the pilot raises the ship a few feet, fall away and stream beneath you. The pilot has already slid back down. I judged we were traveling at a height of about a hundred feet. Sometimes I knew we were lower than that. I didn't know how fast we were going, either. But cars moving along the road at 40 or 50 miles an hour slid rearward rapidly. Going low level. Going low level, as they call it, is the touchstone of the chopper pilot's art, apparently. Shooting a rapids, which I had never done, must be something like this. It was the most exhilarating ride I had ever taken, anywhere. I made three low-level flights while in Vietnam, only one of them necessary, and each time it was the most high-making, hilarity-inducing condition I'd ever tasted. Wasn't this supposed to be dangerous? I could feel a silly, happy grin on my face, as I asked. It was dangerous, the colonel nodded, with a grin back; but it was fun. He stared ahead, his eyes alight. "Breaks up the day." It was also strictly against regulations, unless a situation made it absolutely necessary. What a weird race we were. There was some of the fifth-grader in all of us.

Quang Tri on the Ground

Bulldozers and mine detection crews had cleared space for a prisoner release point beside the river, and from it a road out to the highway for the trucks. The helicopter pad was a quarter mile the other way, to avoid raising the dust, and had its own twisting road through the rubble to the release point. Tent-roofed barracks had been built with separate sections for each of the four-power JMC groups, but all were empty. The North Viets and VC contingents had refused to come, so the Americans and South Viets had not occupied theirs, either. The carefully built, unused, empty barracks seemed symbolic of the entire war and uneasy cease-fire. You felt both sides might suddenly start lobbing shells across the river at each other on the slightest pretext.

The desolation and destruction were eviscerating as we walked on over. Beside the deep powder of the dirt road ruined truck carcasses looked as if they had been hit over and over again, hundreds of larger and smaller fragment holes in their doors and sides. Sharp-looking South Viet soldiers and MPs, styling themselves after the Americans, but looking dusty and grubby in the heat, stood around the truck park in groups. Apparently completely at random, poles were set in the ground to carry larger or smaller South Viet flags which stood out straight, riffling in the breeze. They gave the grim proceedings a circus air, and across the river, with the purplish, gold-starred VC flags, the same circus air prevailed. The Communists had started it with the flags, naturally— my colonel told me—and the South Viets had followed suit. Swept up into piles on the ground were the tire-soled sandals and maroon prisoner uniforms shed by the earlier convoy. I had read in the papers all about the North Viet disrobing routine at the release point; now I was going to see it for myself.

The trucks were not long in coming. The prisoners to be released were trooped across the soft dust of the barren little square of tents and separated into groups of twenty-five, five rows of five. At once they squatted on their heels Oriental-fashion, obedient in their rows. A clear majority of them looked unusually young to my eye. My colonel stood looking at them with his hands on his hips. "Scraping the bottom of the barrel," he said with a grin. One of the Canadian ICCS officers standing nearby looked up and smiled. A Pole nearby stared at us coldly. The remark had been made before, apparently.

It was hard to get any kind of a fix on the prisoners. They stared back at you with set faces, expressionless, or avoided looking at you at all—as you would have done yourself, had you been in their place. Only a very few, usually youngsters, looked the least bit apprehensive or melancholy to be going back. Intelligence had established that they were not being sent home to the North on furlough or to rear-line outfits, but were, once they were re-outfitted and passed through the reception center on the other side, being sent directly to front-line units in the South. Nine or ten had already been recaptured in small fights since the first exchange.

A wry-looking, patient-looking Canadian ICCS colonel standing next to me who spoke Vietnamese offered the information that all of these boys were from the North. All farm boys, very likely. But you could tell they were from the North by their accent. The North Viets had never admitted officially that any of their men or units were fighting in the South, and had gone to great lengths to avoid admitting this in the drafting of the Paris accords, so officially these men were all Viet Cong Southerners.

The disrobing ceremony was clearly prearranged. Whether the first undressing act, which had caused such a furor in the press the very first day, had been spontaneous or not, this one very obviously had been rehearsed. I watched one older soldier in the second group rise up and start taking off his maroon jacket. Then he looked around and saw that he was premature and squatted back down. The rest waiting until one or two leaders in each group rose, and began undressing, and then all the others rose to follow their lead.

They did not take off everything, as I'd been led by the papers to think they would. I thought it would be a much more powerful gesture if they stripped themselves entirely of everything given them by the hated enemy. But they didn't. Without any exceptions they all kept on their purplish-maroon undershorts. Not only that, I noted that without exception they carefully felt around their crotches and the legs of their shorts to make sure nothing of their genitals showed as they squatted back down. I couldn't help feeling this took some of the steam out of the symbolic gesture.

After they had all undressed, they were told by a South Viet officer to march down. And off they went in their groups of twenty-five down to the boats. In the first group, as they started down the dirt incline, one of the leaders who had first disrobed raised his right fist above his head and chanted something. The others, not all of them, but most, raised their fists and chanted the same thing. It sounded to my ear like "Hya-ya hyi!" I asked the Canadian who spoke Viet what they were saying. Oh, he said patiently, just "Down with the American imperialists and their Saigon puppets." Each succeeding group did exactly the same thing at exactly the same place. I stood looking after the boats as they pulled out toward the shallow bar in the middle of the river, where they would have to get out and walk, and I suddenly felt immensely sorry for everybody. The farm boys, the patient Canadian colonel, my American colonel. But that was me. I wasn't sure any of them would have reciprocated.

"You can go across to the other side if you want. They'll feed you some lunch," my colonel said from behind me. "But I can't go. Not allowed."

I stood looking after the boats a moment, shaking my head.

VC

In the tent city on the other side of the river everything was scrupulously clean. And everything went scrupulously by the numbers. Each group of prisoners was met by exactly the same number of monitors, one man for each, who cheered them in unison, rushed into the water to greet them in unison, put their arms around their charges, and in unison marched them up the beach to the tents. Everything was finely organized to clothe them, feed them, and get them through the tent and out the back in the shortest time possible. Other personnel moved around briskly, offering food and tea to newsmen and photographers, politely and cheerfully answering questions, helpfully posing for pictures. A US newsman couldn't be treated nicer anywhere in the world.

Only one hitch occurred. One young prisoner whipped out from inside his shorts a miniature Viet Cong flag he obviously had made and secreted, at great personal risk to himself, while in prison camp. He rather obviously expected to be cheered and congratulated. Perhaps even slapped on the back. Instead, all the monitoring personnel stared at him, obviously nonplused and somewhat aghast. Nobody seemed to know what to do. Finally, one of the monitors snatched the flag and whipped it out of sight, and the young soldier, looking crestfallen, was whisked out the back of the tent out of sight. Without even the meal all his comrades were eating, for all his trouble. And things returned to normal. On the other side of the river other trucks were arriving.

Canadians

Stuck on the islands in the South Pacific back during World War II, we used to have a saying about the Navy SeaBees. We would say, "If I had a beer, a Sea-Bee could have half of it." That was the way you felt about the Canadians in Vietnam.

They knew the score, and they expected nothing better from anybody than what generally happened. They were infallibly correct, infallibly polite, infallibly professional. There was a quiet confidence about them. Perhaps this was because their country had not reached the state yet where their military had to be apologetic about being soldiers. Also, they were tough as nails. They saw through the lies and falsehood of both the NVA and the ARVN. And if the Canadians were ironic and wryly humorous about it, they were also hardheaded as hell. The Poles and Hungarians had been sent there deliberately to be obstructive, to side with the North Viets no matter what, and to inveigh against the ARVN. The Canadians were truly objective. They were also reasonably understanding and tolerant. And resigned. They had done enough of this "peace-keeping" work across the world by now that they seemed to have developed a tradition in their Army about how to handle it.

The Canadians are a fun-loving people. With their Victorian-cum-Calvinist background so similar to ours, this love of fun generally means booze and sex. And occasional head-banging fisticuffs. Naturally this was more noticeable among the younger men— as though the older ones, the colonels, had gone through these particular self-delusions and self-aggrandizements and come out the other side into quiet, less turbulent water with their dignity and self-respect intact.

By comparison, the little, cute, constantly laughing Indonesians with their histories of blood-letting, seemed frivolous. Though they were serious enough. The Poles, with that strong hint of German military sartorial elegance in their uniforms, all seemed to have excessively long aristocratic necks. Apparently chosen for their inability to speak either English or French, they still were not without some humor in their doctrinaire approach. The Hungarians, with no necks at all, and hunched down in their Russian-style, too-tight-in-the-shoulder uniforms, were humorless, spoke nothing, and appeared perpetually red-faced, choked, and petulant. If not in pain.

In Pleiku Mike Healy had invited the four commanders of the Pleiku ICCS team to dinner while I was there, to see about getting me on one of their missions. As Weyand had predicted, the Pole and Hungarian immediately vetoed this. Later in Healy's quarters where the inevitable toasting of everyone's army and everyone's nation took place, Healy who had a good Irish singing voice suddenly suggested each officer sing his country's national anthem. When the five anthems had been sung, Healy turned to a major on his staff, an ex-German who had fought

World War II as a German sergeant, and said, "All right, Fritzie, give us *Deutschland über Alles.*" Fritzie did, and all of it. The big Canadian colonel from Calgary and the diminutive Indonesian thought this was uproariously funny. But the Pole and the Hungarian stiffened and did not laugh. "I'll certainly hear about this from MACV," Healy whispered to me later. "What the hell, I was only trying to teach them a lesson in letting bygones be bygones." The next night at dinner he delivered a long moral lecture on "bygones" when he presented Fritzie his Montagnard knife. But later that same night, when the ICCS were leaving, Healy pulled me to one side and said, "You know, if the NVA and VC don't stop their fooling around, the Canadians are going to pull out of this completely." He had been talking to the big, quiet Calgary colonel. The day before outside Hue a clearly marked ICCS helicopter had been fired on by VC and the American pilot had taken a Chinese AK-47 slug in the thigh. He had just barely managed to get the helicopter back to Hue and land it safely.

In Hue the Hue Canadian team invited me to dinner at the hotel. One of them had just been on the mission on which the American pilot had been hit. They had found out I was interested in the 1968 massacres, and wanted me to meet a Miss Minh who worked for them, and had been through Tet of 1968 and spoke English.

The hotel was typical of war-torn Hue. It was the only "good" one in Hue, was full, had no furnishings at all in the patched-up lobby, and very little furnishings to speak of anywhere else—except for the roof garden restaurant. The restaurant was a different affair, and was run by a private management. It had tables and chairs, honest-to-God tablecloths, and served—the Canadians said—the best "Vietnamese meal" anywhere in South Vietnam. The Canadians loved it. By "Vietnamese" meal they of course meant the kind of gourmet Vietnamese meal you might find in Paris, London or Toronto. I understood that. All the ordinary little local Viet restaurants served you only stir-fried vegetables, rice, chicken and fish. True "Vietnamese cuisine" meals were beyond them, or their resources.

"Wait'll you meet her. Miss Minh," one of the younger Canadians grinned, as I sat with them in their office in the hotel. They were drinking beer. He got up and got himself another beer from the fridge and poured more rye whiskey into it. "Wait'll you hear her talk, man. Man, you won't believe it." That was the tone the evening took.

Miss Minh

She was a stocky flat-faced little girl of maybe nineteen. She had unfortunate teeth, the long heavy exquisite jet-black hair Viet girls have, and eyes that—even when she smiled—had the hard acquisitive luster of black marble buttons. The Canadians had inherited her from some American Army outfit that had pulled out, and with typical loyalty were trying desperately to find her the same kind of clerical job with the US Embassy personnel or Consulate, for after they themselves left. She spoke American English with the stresses and accents of the toughest black Bedford-Stuyvesant ghetto dweller you would ever hope to see.

She had learned it from an American sergeant she had—she sniffed—"worked for" in her office, down at Phu Bai airbase. The Canadians could hardly keep from doubling up when they listened to her. Even when she began to tell her horrendous story of her experiences during Tet of 1968, they had difficulty not laughing.

"Honeh, Ah reckons I don't want eveh see no nothing like that a*gin*. Ne*veh,* in my *whole* life. I hopes *not.*" The thick black gutturals came straight at us out of the flat brown unsmiling Oriental face. She must have had a perfect-pitch ear. Or else her black sergeant had taught her his English with great care —either innocently, or with devilish humor. It was hard not to laugh, but the story wasn't so funny.

"I bout thiteen. They VC, they come take us all to 'at big church. Phu Cam church. That the bishop's church. Put us all in there. Fo' hunned people in there. Can't sit down, can't lay down. They lock us all in there. Two days we ain't got no food." After two days, they let one person from each family out to go home and get food. Miss Minh's father went for them, but did not come back. She talked her way out past a guard, being young, and found her father lying in the yard shot in the leg. She tied up his leg and hid him under the house, and then came back with the food she found. In the church there was nothing but screaming and hollering. People falling down and dying. In all they were in the church five days.

"Them fi' days, they VC, they come take out all the young men and boys. We heah hollering in the street.

They shoot some ob them right there, othehs they march away. We don't see them no more, eveh. The women, they hitting them VC with they fist and a-hollering and yelling for the VC kill them too. They don't care if the VC kill them. Call them pigs, and animals. Me, Ah'm jes tryin' to hide and not get kicked or shot." Finally after five days the women and children were herded out onto the road south to Phu Bai, and told not to stop moving or get off the road, or they would be shot by the guards from the rear. Twice the VC guards fired into them. This was an attempt to stop the American tanks moving up the road toward Hue. "But them tanks, they jes go off ob the road in them fields and keep movin'." She and her mother and two younger sisters had stayed in Phu Bai. After the battle, being the oldest, Minh had come back to Hue to try to find her father but there was no trace of him, and they never heard from him again. Miss Minh assumed the VC had found him under the house and killed him. They had stayed in Phu Bai in the camp for a year. Then she had found her black sergeant and gotten a job with him in his office. He had trained her. And on her salary, they had moved back to their house in Hue. Miss Minh had stayed in Phu Bai until he left. "He say he going to send fo' me come Stateside. He git me a job wif him there. But he neveh do."

"Some story, huh?" one of the younger Canadians said, and dug his chopsticks back into the food. "We're going to find her a job before we leave."

"Take her back with you," I said, and winked at Miss Minh. "Wouldn't you like to go to North America, honey?"

"Thas the onliest place in the world Ah wants to go," Miss Minh said obdurately.

"Sure," the Canadian said, and reached for some more glazed chicken. "You know, we're all straight with her."

Miss Minh stared at both of us with her black marble eyes.

And the rest of us, we sat on, on the hotel roof garden, in the hot night breeze, and the lights of Hue's main street across the river twinkled at us, and the tiny lights from the huge nest of sampans on the river moved rhythmically up and down.

Toilets

It never occurred to me until I got to Hue that toilets would make an interesting cultural study. When you think about it, every nation has its own style of toilet, and even its own evolution of toilet styles. The British upper-class toilet, for example, is distinctive and like no other toilet in the world, including the British lower-class toilet. It is capacious, its large bowl grand and deluxe in its heavy, elegant simplicity, and it sits solid and sturdy on its floor. All the rich people I know in Europe have it. The first thing they do when they move into a house is remove all the existing toilets and install the British upper-class one.

All the toilets I saw in Hue were turn-of-the-century French. A heavy cast-iron box up near the ceiling. From which a soft-lead pipe runs down to the bowl. A long chain with a wooden handle hangs from the box, the handle usually missing. The bowl can hardly be called a bowl. It is more an elongated, truncated cone, too tall for its diameter so that it looks like it might fall over, straight up and down so that it provides a straight chute. When you pulled the chain, the action was heavy and turgid, as though all the inside parts were still made of cast iron too. A flat, unrounded, uncomfortable wood seat completed the ensemble.

I first noticed this phenomenon when I was visiting the Hue MACV compound and needed a toilet. I had just come from Pleiku where in Healy's compound built by Americans, naturally only American toilets were installed. I was startled to see old-style French toilets in an American installation. Of course MACV Hue was in a French building, built by the French, probably around the end of the 1940s. My toilet in the Continental Palace in Saigon was the same, but coming straight from Paris as I had, I hadn't noticed.

Like all 19th-century toilets, the French 19th-century toilet was built to last but that was about all you could say for it. Beauty, esthetics, gaiety—all those French *fin-de-siècle* characteristics—were not part of it. It was certainly not something you would want to sit on and read a book. In spite of that, with typical French originality, the French went right on making and installing it while other nations revamped their toilet concepts. They went right on producing it, in fact, up until after World War II when the American economic influence began to be felt, at which point they began making cheap bad copies of American toilets.

After that first revelation in the Hue MACV latrine, I began looking around and taking note. Not only in Hue, but in Saigon. In Da Nang, Nha Trang, everywhere I went. Almost nowhere were there modern French toilets.

It seemed to me emblematic of the whole cultural and industrial three-card-monte con game the French had played not only on their Annamese cousins, but upon themselves.

Hue Survivors

There seems to be no question that the NVA-VC high command knew all along they could not expect to hold Hue more than a couple of weeks or a month. If they thought so, it indicated a naiveté on their part that is incredible. But they may have been victims of their own propaganda, and *believed* the people would rise up and throw off the yoke of the Saigon puppets. Certainly the Communist rank and file believed it, and were led to believe it. Which indicated a gullibility and simple-mindedness among the rank and file that is equally as incredible. At least to a Westerner.

The Communists held large, and then increasingly smaller, parts of Hue from dawn of January 31st to February 25th. The killings began almost immediately. With fighting going on all around them, known Americans and other foreigners were rounded up by teams led by officers carrying clipboards holding lists of names. Those who tried to resist arrest were shot in the head on the spot. Those who surrendered were led away with their arms wired together behind their backs, and have never been heard of again. Some bodies were recovered. None were on the later POW lists.

But the killings did not stop there. In Gia Hoi, the northeast residential section, which the Allied command decided to leave till last because it had no important objectives, and which the Communists held for the full twenty-five days, announcements, calls, arrests, disappearances and outright killings in the street went on continuously and in sporadic bursts. Things centered around the Gia Hoi High School. The Communist headquarters were in a private house nearby. Meetings were held in the school's yard; certain executions were done in the yard under a big fruit tree. Men walked the streets with megaphones, announcing that at least one adult from each family should report to the school. Many people hid. Communist search teams hunted some of them down, left others inexplicably alone. At first, people thought the government troops would come right back in and free them. Then as the days passed, thought they might never come back. Then, beginning on February 22nd, the searches and arrests began to increase. Apparently the Viet Cong and NVA had finally realized they were going to lose the town. Whole groups of people were marched away, not to be seen again. One Viet woman, who had hidden six male members of her family, some of them soldiers, for the full twenty-three days, saw them taken away with their arms wired behind them, now that the VC were leaving. Later she found all six bodies, shot in the head, in the high school yard.

All told, I interviewed ten or twelve survivors of Hue. All had lost relatives or immediate family. All had barely escaped with their lives, by hiding, or by lying, or by staying out of sight and finally running away to friends in another part of the town. Finally, the stories became so similar and predictable they no longer added anything new. And I found myself beginning to get bored with them. I could no longer participate in feeling their terror with them. One woman talked about seeing the German medical team led away, and I thought of Hilary Smith in Kontum. Dr. Krainick, and his wife, Elizabeth, and two other neutral German doctors. Mrs. Krainick yelled at the guards not to touch her husband as they were taken away. That was on the fifth day. The four executed bodies were later found buried in a field on the edge of town. A man told of the owner of Hue's best-known "Chinese soup" shop. Four armed men, he thought North Viets, came to the shop at four in the afternoon and ordered "Chinese soup." After they drank the soup, they arrested the owner for being a spy, wired his arms, and started to take him away. When he resisted, one of them shot him in the head in the doorway of his shop.

With my interpreter I visited the melancholy Gia Hoi High School playground, where so many executions and burials had taken place, and visited the "Strawberry Patch" on the outskirts of Gia Hoi where so many of the bodies had been buried. Then we drove out past the Phu Cam cathedral far out of town to the south, to see the huge official mass grave to which most of the bodies had been removed and the bones from the salt flats and mountains had been added, all of them now legitimate political capital for the South Viet government. So many corpses, killed at the same time, buried in the same place, was somehow stupefying in the fierce sun, and there was no shade.

An association had been formed in Hue called the Association for the Preservation of the Memory of the Victims of Tet 1968, and my interpreter Vo arranged for me to meet with them. We drove out to a private house in the Gia Hoi section for the meeting.

The Gia Hoi streets were wide and there were pretty, old houses in the area with big yards, but nothing much grew in the yards and the trees looked starved for water. The whole place would turn into a mud hole in the rainy season. The overpowering heat and the dust made it a job even to turn the steering wheel and work the brake. I felt weak in the legs and half sick. I tried to imagine NVA cadres walking the streets with megaphones. It made my hackles rise. So I was in a good mood for the meeting.

The chairman of the committee was a young man in a lightweight business suit, clearly a townie. The other four men—the president, secretary, treasurer and vice-president—sat in straight-backed chairs along the walk and all wore fresh-laundered white shirts and no ties. They were all clearly farmers and not at home in their shoes and socks. They all seemed pleased and surprised a Western reporter would want to talk about 1968. They gave us the list of people to interview that we had come for, and Vo wrote it down. The chairman's father had been a victim. All the others had lost immediate family—brothers, fathers, sons. They told me the Communists when leaving had formed three columns, one to the west, one south, one north. In Phu Thu district an ARVN unit had found the first corpse. Villagers had spread out, found many more. Most were tied with elbows behind them. Not shot. Hit with pick handles. In Phu Thu there were 1074 bodies. In Nam Hoa people were found in a "brook." Estimate 379, by counting skulls. But the skulls drifted along the "brook." Their association was formed to take care of the cemeteries. Also to look after the families who were destitute. The association was asking the JMC to try and get from the NVA their prisoner lists, and to tell where the rest were buried. Their families were very important to them as Buddhists, and proper Buddhist burial was important to Buddhists. Many of the graves that had been found had been found through people who had survived the massacres, who had been clubbed but hadn't died, who had been buried but had crawled out. So far they had had little luck with the North Viet delegation, who were now in Saigon. After another cup of tea and another handshaking ceremony all around, we left them and drove back to the river in the heat. It all sounded so hopeless.

Later I found out from my American JMC colonel at MACV that this same association was the group who a week before had organized and perpetrated the riot and stoning of the North Viet delegation to the JMC, and caused their return to Saigon. Obviously, with government connivance, the colonel grinned. Or they couldn't have gotten away with it. I nodded, and agreed. But I didn't know how to fit in this new piece of information. The South Viet MPs and guards had simply stood by and watched when the crowd mobbed the North Viets. He had nearly gotten hit with a rock himself, fighting to protect the North Viets, the colonel laughed. How to judge that, I wondered. And did that make my committee insincere? Were they on the government payroll? And did that nullify the killings? "Come on," the JMC colonel said, taking pity on my distress, "I'll buy you a drink. Don't try to understand this country. I've been out here four one-year tours, and I don't."

Cô Van

She worked at MACV in Hue. Cô in Vietnamese means "Miss." Miss Van. Nobody at MACV Hue ever called her anything else. Cô Van spoke English and the JMC colonel thought she might be able to translate for me in Hue at least, because I was having trouble with my Saigon interpreter Vo.

My problem with Vo wasn't major but it was enough to upset things. The main thing was that Vo's French was as bad as mine, and I couldn't get him to speak English. He would make gross mistakes in French, which my French wasn't good enough to catch, and we would have to have these long discussions in the middle of an interview about whether a person had said this, or that. Also he had a distressing habit of condensation. A person I was interviewing would talk on and on in Vietnamese, and Vo would look at the wall a moment and give me the gist of it in one succinct French sentence. "She went down town, and bought some vegetables, and she came back home." I could not get it through to him that the details were what I wanted.

That was how I came to meet Cô Van.

Cô Van was tall for a Viet girl, which meant she came up almost to my shoulder. She seemed to have a not-bad figure, but it was hard to tell in an *ao-dai*. And she smiled evasively and self-effacingly all the time. She was polite to the point of saccharinity. I soon learned this self-effacement covered a vanity at least as hard and great as Ernest Hemingway's. The JMC colonel, grinning, called her a 24-year-old virgin spinster. None of his young men at MACV had been able to get to first base with her, first base here being a single date.

I used her as an interpreter for one afternoon. The result was such a catastrophe that I quickly gave up the idea of annulling my marriage to Mr. Vo. She took me to two shops in town chosen at random, one a shoeshop, the other a cutlery place. The one tried to sell me shoes, and the other tried to sell me cutlery. Then she took me out to Tay Loc suburb in the west of the Citadel, through which the Viet Cong had passed in their first attack, to visit a peasant family which apparently had once worked for her father. The peasant family, now all of them together running a little sandal-making shop, were so effusive with us that they would say no more than Yes, yes, they hated the Viet Cong. Though they had not seen them on their way through. Also I discovered Cô Van's English was not all that good, outside the usage of her MACV job. After all of that, driving back, Cô Van told me sweetly that she would have been glad to translate more for me if I had only had more to say. Then she invited me to her home for tea or a drink because her father would like to meet me. (Later, the JMC colonel told me that to MACV's knowledge I was the only American Cô Van had ever so invited.)

I went. I was fascinated. We drove out south from the river bridge along the main road. This was the road to Phu Bai, the road Miss Minh's group had taken during Tet 1968, at VC gun point. I wondered how Cô Van would have done in Minh's group. When we got quite far out, Cô Van indicated I should turn off to the right. As soon as I did, the area began immediately to look considerably poorer. The houses were not shacks or hovels, but all of them were ramshackle and had clearly seen better days. Cô Van immediately began to apologize for the area.

I asked her if she had been in Hue at the time of Tet. She said no, she hadn't. Fortunately she had been in Saigon going to university. But her family had been here; they had stayed hidden except for her mother who went out to get food and nothing had happened to them. I asked her what she was going to do when the Americans left. She smiled and hung her head and said she did not know. She hoped to get a job with the American Consulate. The colonel had said he would help her. I asked what she would do if the Communists came back. She said she did not know. She hoped they wouldn't. Anyway, she did not think the Americans would let the Communists come back. In any case, that was what she chose to believe; it was the only thing she could believe. If the Communists came back, she would certainly go to prison since she had worked for my people. She did not say this accusingly exactly, and smiled her sweet smile at me. When we came to her home, she pointed where I should turn in, and began to apologize for the poorness of it and of the neighborhood.

It was certainly a poor-looking place, for a girl as clean and as all together as Cô Van. For our afternoon of interviewing she had taken off the *ao-dai* and put on a Western dress. She looked quite grand. I pulled the car inside a hanging, nonfunctioning steel gate. They had not always lived here, Cô Van said. Her father had been a mandarin. A university professor, way back. Then he had worked in the government for President Diem's brother. During that time they had had a nice house in the good part of Gia Hoi. But then he had been asked to work in the elections for President Diem's brother, and had refused because he did not like the candidates. He had lost his job, and the Gia Hoi house had been taken away and given to his successor. Since then he had not worked because there was very little that he could do. He only knew how to teach, or work in a government office. Such a man could not take a menial, inferior job. Since then they had lived here. Cô Van smiled sweetly at the low-roofed, unpleasant, dilapidated house. She, Cô Van, now supported all of them.

I parked the car inside the court. Pigs and chickens grunted and squawked and ran from it. Four houses formed the three sides of the court. Two low fleshy tropical trees grew in the court, making some shade over the dust, but not much. In the center of the court was a huge rusting pile of old automobile carcasses and pieces, one of them an old US Army truck without wheels or doors or hood. We walked to the house through the deep dust and the smell of chickens and pigs. Cô Van informed me sweetly that they were not her family's chickens and pigs. Nor was the junk.

Inside, it was relatively cool. I saw nothing of it but a big, dark living room—and part of a very primitive kitchen beyond. On a once expensive couch sat Cô Van's father. He was a thin, faded man with enormous cheekbones and enormous hollows under them. When he stood up to be introduced he barely came up to my diaphragm. Pleased to learn I spoke French, he sat back down and in French immediately began to address me on American literature, about which he knew little. He spoke no English. He had read *Tant qu'il y aura des hommes (From Here to Eternity* in French), long ago, and remembered it well. Though he did not agree with everything in it. Then he told me he was a Catholic, and asked me if I believed in God.

So we talked about God, and the Bible, and theology, and the universe, and mysticism for about an hour. I ran out of gas after twenty minutes because I could not get him on anything but an old-fashioned doctrinaire Catholic approach. He had not, for example, read Teilhard de Chardin. But the old man kept right on, unaware in his thirsty verbal web-spinning that he had lost his audience. Cô Van sat in her chair, smiling primly at first one of us, then the other. And going to the kitchen to get us tea and beer from her mother. From the kitchen door the worn rotund woman in black pajamas with her hair skinned back in a bun kept darting quick looks in at us with a half snarl, as if calculating how much work we were making for her by sitting there smoking and talking about God and drinking tea and beer. After an hour of it I stood up.

It was still only late afternoon. On the way back to MACV Cô Van, expanding, unlimbered a little. What she really wanted, more than anything, more than anything in her life, was to go to the United States and study. She had been hoping that someone would offer to sponsor her, but so far no one had offered. I didn't offer, either. But I asked her what she would like to study. She said she would like to teach history in the United States, perhaps in an American high school. Failing that, she would like to study pharmacy. In Vietnam a pharmacist was a very important and valuable part of the society. Much more so than in the United States or Europe, she understood. To have a pharmacy in Vietnam was a very fine business. Did I not think that a worthwhile project? I said I thought I did.

Back at the MACV compound Cô Van held out her hand to me to be shaken. As if she were doing me yet another favor. So I shook it. Then she walked away from me, her hips swaying, Oriental-fashion. I shook my head. I had seen it but I still found it hard to believe.

Dak Pek A Third Time

I had had it with Hue. And I felt Hue had about had it with me. I had spent nearly a week there, and I was ready to move on. But I had not heard from Healy about the Dak Pek trip. Finally, I put in a call to him.

After twenty minutes of trying, Healy finally came on the line. The frustrated operator had finally had to go through the Army system in Saigon to get Pleiku. Healy and I shouted at each other over the static on the line. Over and over in my notes, later on, I found entries about the lousy state of the phone system in Vietnam. The enormous growth that came with the American incursion had put an immense strain on the already poor system. The difficulty of stringing lines and keeping them open in the disruptions of a hostile countryside had added to this. It was actually easier to call the United States from Pleiku than to call Hue.

Healy shouted that he hadn't called because he had nothing to report. For the moment, the Dak Pek trip was off. He had thought he had figured out a way to go without being given a direct order to stop. He just wouldn't inform the JMC until we were already airborne. He had been very excited about it. He had about decided to go along himself. So he had thought we were going. But it just wasn't possible. We simply could not go in unilaterally. Not that far. A mechanical failure would be catastrophic. To go down deep in VC country. If the chase ship failed in its pick-up, facilities were no longer available to seal off the area. He did not have to tell me what kind of repercussions that would have. The only way we could go in now was in conjunction with a resupply by Chinook hooks. We had talked about the disadvantages of that, but he thought he had figured out a way around some of them. Colonel Black was trying to set that up for some future date. Old Charlie was pretty excited about going, too. He thought they might be able to set it up and know for sure some time before I left Vietnam. Meantime, why didn't I go on down to Da Nang and poke around there a day or two? It would be just as easy to fly me back to Pleiku from Da Nang as from Hue. He would call General Hiestand in Da Nang and tell him I was coming. As far as that went, it would be just as easy to fly me back up from Saigon for it, if I returned to Saigon before Charlie Black got it set up.

On my end of the line I felt disappointment flooding all over me. I didn't really know, had not yet made up my mind, how long I was going to stay in Vietnam. That they might not organize the trip until after I left, and then go ahead and make it, was more than I wanted to think about. I didn't know why the idea of that trip had gotten under my skin so—or perhaps I did know. But anyway, it had. On the other hand, I was beginning to feel I was using Healy's friendship for me, and I did not want to do that.

On the phone Mike was shouting something about General Hiestand. Hiestand was Mike's counterpart in I Corps (they still pronounced it "Eye" Corps), and the advisor to the famous General Truong who had fought at Hue and now commanded I Corps for the South Viets. He's not like me, Hiestand, Mike shouted and I could hear the grin in his voice. He's just the least bit more—uh—formal.

I said I didn't mind that. But I had to grin. When I hung up, I found Mike had somehow managed to reinstall in me a perhaps feeble but nonetheless viable confidence that I would still get to see Dak Pek.

Driving to Da Nang

It was sixty miles. Sixty miles straight down the coast. This was the famous Highway No. 1, the "Street Without Joy" of Bernard Fall. Four or five stretches along

Route 1 had claimed the famous name, until now the whole highway from Hue to Saigon was called "Street Without Joy." (The true "Street Without Joy" was between Hue and Quang Tri, east of Route 1, which I'd flown over by helicopter going up to view the prisoner release.) About the only section of Route 1 which anyone would declare totally and completely open to civilian traffic—although it took occasional long-distance mortarings from the VC—was the stretch from Hue to Da Nang, and I wanted to see it.

The same American colonel who had loaned me his jeep for the Buddhist funeral suggested I take it again for the trip. If I insisted on making it. He was prepared to fly me down. This time, instead of the driver, the young ARVN captain drove the jeep himself. A two-hour drive. It would be a good opportunity, the American colonel explained, for the captain to visit his wife and stay overnight, since he lived in Da Nang. Unbeknown to the colonel and me, the captain —after asking my interpreter Vo how nice a guy I was —had also arranged to pick up the three of his four small children who were going to school in Hue and staying with relatives. These were standing waiting out of sight of the colonel around the corner from the compound. So it was Captain Tri, me, Vo, and the three children in the jeep as we left Hue. I felt like a platoon commander.

For the first ten miles down to Phu Bai the traffic was choked and the dust heavy. A continuous unbroken string of villages, hamlets, houses and shacks lined both sides of the road. And everywhere there were soldiers. Military posts and road-guard bunkers, with their inevitable South Viet flag on its pole, were built-in every few hundred yards. Then it began to thin out and the countryside became visible now and then. For a long time we drove alongside the huge, shallow Dam Cau Hai bay. Inland, the forested mountains with their thick football shoulders came right down onto the flat, two miles away.

It was fantastically beautiful country. Or would have been, if it had not been for the war. Across the dun flatlands dozens of streams and rivers outlined in greenery moved from the feet of the mountains to the water of the great bay. Little three- and four-house hamlets and single farm dwellings crouched under their canopies of coco palm and fleshy fan-leafed banana plants in the flat dun landscape. Water buffaloes and cone-hatted people moved with tropical lassitude in the dun heat-shimmering fields.

But each hamlet had its protective machinegun bunker and accordion wire, each single house its wire and red-striped yellow flag, each road its concertina roadblocks, each river its strung-wire water-traffic blocks and sentries along the banks.

Each bridge we crossed now had roadblocks at both ends, encroaching out onto the blacktop to narrow the highway to a single lane, their double and triple concertinas thrown back to leave the road open. They would all be closed at nightfall, Captain Tri told me through Vo. Sentries at both ends directed the alternating traffic through. The larger bridges had bunkers at both ends and searchlights mounted on their railings pointing inland. Armed men patrolled them. Each three-house hamlet along the highway had its own roadblocks, and lone guards sat in homemade sentry boxes with a piece of tin over the top to keep off the sun.

A pervasive feeling of unease began to circulate in

the jeep. I looked around and tried to spot where it was coming from. It seemed to be coming from Captain Tri, but it infected Vo, and even the children. In the long straight open stretches without bridges or villages everyone in the jeep got very quiet. I started to whistle suddenly and looked around at them with a grin. It made everyone grin back and the children laughed. But I couldn't keep them there. The unease seeped back.

And that was the way it stayed all the way down the coast, past the other big bay of Dam Lap An, where the highway runs out on a long thin spit between the bay and the sea, crossing the narrow mouth on a bridge at Lang Co, and then on to the great Da Nang pass we had been looking at ahead of us for over an hour. We stopped in Lang Co for a "Chinese soup" and an ice cream for the children, at a tiny open-front soup shop frequented by soldiers on the tree-shaded main street, and Tri and Vo relaxed. Then we pushed on, Captain Tri gripping the wheel tighter and pushing harder at the accelerator, to the top of the spectacular pass. At the top of the pass was a Viet roadhouse and soup shop, startlingly like the road-houses-filling stations at the tops of all the other passes I had crossed, in the Alps or the Rockies, and we stopped a few minutes and looked far down the other side at Da Nang sending a great cloud of smoke and dust up to pollute the clear air. But Captain Tri was edgy and wanted to keep on. When we were finally in the smoky outskirts of Da Nang, he at last sat back and gave me a grin.

I winked back at him, but I found it hard to understand. If the trip made him that edgy, why subject his three small children to it? If it was that dangerous, why take a chance with his own children's lives? Later I asked Vo, and Vo smiled. The children had not seen their mother since the last school vacation. And would not see her again until the next one. Even then, someone would have to make the trip. In one direction or the other. Besides, it wasn't really dangerous, only potentially so. I must remember that this was their way of life. And that they were used to it. Why not bring the children? Two generations in Vietnam had grown up like this. They didn't know any other way of life.

The Pass of Clouds

I had been told in both Saigon and Hue that the drive to Da Nang was worth it if only to see and travel the pass. I didn't remember its Viet name, but translated directly into French it became *le col des nuages*. Shortened into common US Army language—which never used a word it could avoid (excepting, of course, one)—it became Cloud Pass. Not an ugly name, either, reminiscent of Indians and the Rockies and the Frontier.

It was visible along the coast for a very long way in both directions. At Nui Ai Van the mountains came right down to the sea in a long majestic sweep of many ridges, thrusting right out into the sea itself in an irregular two-mile peninsula. The road ran up over the saddle of the peninsula, two thousand feet above the sea, and was a superb feat of old-time engineering. Crossing ridge after ridge of forest, bending back on itself again and again to fight for and gain the height it needed to sweep into the saddle, it was an awesome sight from miles away and presented a hundred breath-taking views down on the sea. On the Da Nang side it was easier, dropping swiftly down one immense long irregular ridge shoulder to the flatlands, but the sight was as awesome as on the Hue side.

Some local meteorological phenomenon caused low-lying layers of cumulus cloud to perpetually cover the peaks inland, and hang on the upper slopes above the pass. As with all of the grand or bizarre natural phenomena of Vietnam, the old Vietnamese had attached a magic to the place, and a ghost was supposed to inhabit the cloud-covered upper slopes. Coming up the tortuous, twisting, puny path over and around the great ridges, or rolling cautiously down the insignificant thread along the gigantic mountain shoulder on the Da Nang side, it was easy to believe a ghost inimical to man lived up above. The nature stillness and enormous mountain quiet that seeped down from the hanging cloud cover and rolled like gelatin down the jungled slopes seemed to be the ghost-god's warning portent of silence to the entire race of man. Up there, all of our irascible scrambling and biting shrank to unimportance.

It appeared to have been a battleground at some time in the past, and apparently had been defoliated. Tall bare hardwood trunks thrust up out of the green sparsely here and there. It was easy to imagine the VC coming down from the cloud cover, through the jungle growth. Now everything had grown back, as lushly as before, except for the tall admonitory fingers of the dead hardwoods. And already long slender saplings were pushing up to compete with them. On the way down to Da Nang I asked what kept the VC from coming down and knocking off the present roadhouse in the pass. Both Tri and Vo grinned. "They pay," Vo said.

Da Nang

If Da Nang resembled a smoky scab on the fair skin of Vietnam from the Nui Ai Van pass, it was worse when you got down close to it and into it. A thick dust from the heavy military traffic made the air unbreathable in the fading sun of late afternoon. The acrid smoke of huge trash and garbage fires permeated the dust and spread with it. With its natural harbor for unloading, its great storage parks for matériel, nowhere that I saw in Vietnam did the inroads of the US industrial invasion show a more devastating face or create such havoc, for what must once have been a pretty, sleepy port town. I was totally disoriented, so I had no idea where we were going, but at one point Tri drove across water over a causeway that was still in process of being built on a fill of garbage. US Army trucks were unloading on it as we passed. A dozen garbage fires sent streams of garbage smoke straight up in the air. Tri and Vo shook their heads. I felt myself flushing. I had no way of telling them, it was too difficult, that they were looking at an example of the American Way. Utilize

the muck and detritus of life to make something useful. Eventually good clean dirt would cover the garbage and smother the smell. And *voilà!* An American
legacy for Da Nang. Only, it looked like now the
Americans weren't going to be there long enough to
make enough garbage to finish the job.

About the only pretty place I saw in Da Nang was
the MACV compound across the river from the town.
The river is an important presence in Da Nang. More
so, it seemed to me, than in Saigon or Hue. Settings of
trees and plantings of grass had made the compound
pleasant and relatively cool on its bank of the long
spit the river made between itself and the sea. If you
half shut your eyes, the wide river became one of
those ancient, broad, slow-moving Conradian rivers
of the 19th-century Conradian Orient. Sampans and
ships moved slowly up and down it. And the eyesore
on the other side became a sleepy village. Here the
American advisory command could live in relative
comfort, and not think about the mess we had made
of Da Nang on the other side. Although they still had
to drive through the town to get from their offices to
the river bridge.

Nickel, Dime, Quarter

I was invited to have dinner with General Hiestand
the first night I was there. Hiestand's mess was at the
same time both less formal, and much more austere,
than Mike Healy's. There was no formal General's

Mess in a room apart. Hiestand and a few of his top-ranking staff officers sat at a big round table with his guests, and in a pattern of ever widening concentric circles at other tables came the lower field-grade officers and then the junior and more junior officers. One noted right away that the laughter was most hushed and quiet at the farthest tables. In the end, it was probably only a matter of personal style. Hiestand himself was a tall, gray-haired man with bright eyes and a wry smile, and very reserved. Later one of his colonels said to me, "You'd never know he wasn't a West Pointer, would you? He's more Point than the Pointers. He's an OCS, just like me. But he's one hell of a good soldier." He was obviously a superb administrator. We ate a stir-fried Korean beef dish with some obscure fruit diced up in it, the recipe for which Hiestand said wryly was the only souvenir he brought out of Korea. It was a fantastic dish. Almost worth a trip to Korea. It felt strange to be eating it with a fork instead of sticks, after my last few days with Vo. After the meal, there was the nightly movie in the bar. But a poker game immediately got started at a round table in a corner of the big mess.

I was invited to sit in. Urged to, even. Though it didn't take much urging. I knew even before I sat down that I was being tested. They didn't need a college literary board to test me. They had their own test. It was only a small game of nickel, dime and quarter, but that didn't matter. I was having my credentials checked. Quite a crowd gathered and hung over the table for the first hour. Most of the talk around the table was about the final pull-out on March 29th. (X +60 had been put back one day, when the North Viets held up the second POW list.) In Da Nang they were getting seriously understaffed on personnel, and overstocked on food. The mess officer was trying to give steaks away. Just about every man was holding down at least two jobs. Everybody was looking forward to the end, and going home. There was a long discussion about the bombings of the North at the end of the past year. Several younger officers thought the US had hurt its international reputation seriously, quite apart from any humanitarian aspects. The older officers were more cynical. "Look. It's all a poker game. Just like right here," one of them said amiably. "With all of our troops already moved out of here, what did we have to call them with, except our Air? They never would have signed the cease-fire." He picked up his cards. "You take old Uncle Ho and Pham Van Dong and sit them down here and teach them the game, and inside of a week they'd be taking all the money." Everyone was concerned about the POWs, and everyone had at least one friend who was a prisoner.

We played until four in the morning. Then all made our own breakfast in the mess hall kitchen. I wound up with scrambled eggs and one of the big thick steaks the mess officer was having difficulty getting rid of. It all seemed incredibly rich, with its bank of stainless-steel stoves and platoon of freezers, compared to what was across the river.

In the final accounting it showed up that I was thirty dollars behind. The truth was, I had gotten so interested in their discussions of Vietnam and their nostalgic anecdotes that I had forgotten to play. The game currency was the official Military Payment Certificate (MPC) script (which was being turned in for real dollars in two or three days, all over South Viet-

nam) and I suffered so much razzing that finally I
pulled out my wallet and showed them the ten-dollar,
five-dollar, and one one-dollar MPC bills I had put
away to take home to my son in Paris for his money
collection. That brought my losses down to fourteen
dollars. It did not remove the stigma. My poker loss at
Da Nang would precede me everywhere I traveled in
Vietnam afterward. Even down into the Delta. They
even heard about it at the *Times* Saigon bureau. But
I would get revenge in Pleiku.

Guilt

With the others all gone to bed at four-thirty in the
morning, I sat on the concrete bunker by the river's
edge and watched first light come up. I was suffering
a severe attack of what, for lack of a better word, I had
come to call guilt-panic.

As always, the light seemed to seep down from the
sky from no visible source, gradually etching in gray
objects that night for a while had rendered nonexist-
ent. Across the broad river, Da Nang was not yet clear
enough to be visible.

There was no possibility of sleep. I had never been
able to isolate exactly what caused these attacks. But
I had been getting them all my life since I was a boy.
The symptoms were similar to fear. But different in
the way they tasted. The mind kept darting around
like a rat in a box. There was a nervous tic in the area
of the diaphragm that made it hard to breathe. The

thighs and ankles felt tight and twitchy as though they wanted me to get up and run. But here there was no physical object as there was in fear, no danger point to concentrate on, no action to enact. I could sit here and calmly, coolly analyze the reactions I was having, but I couldn't make them go away. As always, I had the feeling I had as a boy, of wanting to cry, "I'm sorry, God, I'm sorry." Although I no longer believed in that kind of a God. I knew the attacks well enough to know there was nothing to do with them but sit with them, and wait them out. Eventually they would wear themselves out and go away. And then it would stop.

While I waited, I tried to figure out what could be behind this one. The obvious answer of course was Vietnam. But I didn't feel guilty about Vietnam. Anyway, these attacks never came from anything specific. They were general. Maybe I felt guilty about humanity. About, even, being a member of humanity. But all the other answers were too simple. I had been to the refugee camps, and had visited them, and knew about them. Everybody knew about them. There wasn't even anything new to write about them. They were still there. The North accused the South of creating them deliberately. The South accused the North of the same thing. In any case, just living in a war zone would create refugees. And refugees had to live in refugee camps. Maybe it was just the fact that I had so much enjoyed eating such a good breakfast of scrambled eggs and steak. But the attacks never came for simple, clear reasons like that. I supposed, I guessed—again—that humanity was the cause. Again. Like always. A sense of the backwardness of humanity. Of the cruelty, the indifference, the Kantian solipsism humanity mostly consisted of. It made a terrible despair.

After twenty minutes I could feel the seizure beginning to slack off. The false dawn of first light had gone, replaced by real dawn. Across the river the buildings along the river's bank were clearly visible. The garbage fires still sent streams of smoke straight up in the air.

After a few minutes of just breathing, I got up and went inside.

Movies

Certain intellectual American writers who have never fought wars away from home have written rather caustically over the years about the plethora of American films shown to our military personnel in Vietnam. They have pointed out the low cultural level of such films, and have drawn disquieting conclusions from this about the lamentable general state of our culture. I couldn't agree more.

But they also dwelt on the unseemliness, the downright indecency, of treating our troopers to such luxuries as films—and feeding them ice cream and soda pop and beer—in the midst of a poor underdeveloped country where most people barely have enough to eat. And I thought this was a bit too much.

In the first place, I didn't find the South Vietnamese as a whole all that hungry. Except for the poor, the refugees, the beggars and the crippled war veterans,

I found them pretty well off. In the second place, I never saw any Vietnamese who if he had something, would refuse to eat it or rub it on himself or sell it, just because an American or another Vietnamese did not have it.

I saw a lot of films while I was in Vietnam, mainly because around US military installations there isn't anybody to talk to during the time the evening film is run. Their cultural level was certainly low. So was their artistic level, their esthetic level, their philosophical level and, worst, their entertainment level. This is not to say, however, as the intellectual writers seemed to think, that the officers and men who went to them so religiously night after night went like cattle, to sit bemused and stupefied. They went mainly to laugh at the stupidities they were being offered. The house was more often filled with whistles and groans than not. They had their own lively esthetic and their own lively critical sense, which mainly was whether what they were watching had anything to do with life as they had experienced it. Implausible plot lines, fuzzy characterization, unmotivated love scenes; they saw through them all. They had their own sardonic audience rating, which was Skin 1, Skin 2, Skin 3 depending on the amount of flesh shown; and Fuzz 1, Fuzz 2, depending on the amount of pubic hair. Skin 3, Fuzz 2—like *Music Lovers,* for example—was tops.

But mainly I think they went so they would not be alone, not have to think. During those evening hours. In Pleiku, in Can Tho, in Tay Ninh, in Hue, even in Saigon, it's hard to sit in your room and study culture night after night. Remembering back, and all the lousy movies I went to during three years as a wartime soldier, it is difficult to judge now—though I hated them all at the time—just how much of my precarious sanity was saved by them. So it may be hard for intellectual writers to judge just how many bone-cold souls our low-culture film industry in Vietnam has saved from terminal frostbite. A lot depends on your point of view, and where you're sitting.

I went to see Milos Foreman's *Taking Off* with General Hiestand in Da Nang. I was curious about the reaction it would get, since I had already seen it. I was irritated because in the scene where the unlovely girl hippie sings the song about "fuck everything," the Vietnam version used a whistle-beep instead of the word itself. In the Paris English-language version the girl sang the word, and her inflection made the whole scene much funnier, more ridiculous. And I had wanted to see the local Army reaction to it.

In any case, when it was over, General Hiestand stood up and adjusted his sport shirt as if it were a blouse, and said wryly, "Well, if that's the way things are back home, maybe it's a good thing we're over here."

"Don't you believe it, Sir!" a young major's clear boyish voice said from the rear. "We'll take anything we can get!" And the place broke up into laughter.

Over My Lai

General Truong the I Corps commander was making an inspection tour of some outlying Border Ranger posts the next day. General Hiestand asked me if I would like to go along.

Lt General Ngo Quand Truong had first become known to the American public when as a brigadier he commanded the 1st South Viet Division which had held out in the Citadel of Hue during the 1968 Tet Offensive. In 1972 he became famous again when he took over command in Hue and stopped the Communist push at My Chanh and drove them back to Quang Tri. It was then he gave his famous order, much publicized in the American press, that all deserters found in Hue after a twenty-four-hour period would be shot out of hand. Young for his rank, Truong was a small man, even for a Vietnamese, slight and slender, with slightly hunched shoulders and an enormous intensity about him. He appeared to me to be a basically shy man who had learned to control his shyness with an iron will. He was very good-looking. He had large, somewhat bulging, liquid eyes with a deceptive gentleness in them, which seemed to look straight out at the world with an eager, boyish interest as if seeking any information from whatever source that might be of aid to him. He was a rarity among South Vietnamese generals, in that he apparently had no political ambitions at all, and in that he was not lucratively engaged in the cinnamon business or the teak business, or any other business. He was apparently just exactly what he wanted to be, a soldier. In all the times that I saw him I never knew him to smile.

Two of the posts he was visiting far out in the Song Vu Gia valley, Hiestand explained, had been receiving North Viet .122 artillery fire in the past two days, and Truong wanted to see what was going on. Then we would visit another post forty miles south, go on to Quang Ngai for lunch and a consultation with the divisional commander there, come back via the coast and land at An Hai where two Regional Forces soldiers had been killed last night in a mortaring attack, and then fly back to Da Nang along the coast. A trip of some two hundred twenty miles. I, who had just used two hours plus to drive the sixty miles from Hue, was always a little unprepared for the unbelievable distances a helicopter could cover. We would also be flying over My Lai, Hiestand said with a wry, enigmatic smile.

In my turn, I wondered why Hiestand even had told me, because if he hadn't I would never have known.

I was an old hand at helicopters by now. And I was familiar with the customary layout of a Border Ranger firebase post. I had flown over enough of them. All the ones we visited were the conventional shapes, their mortar pits and artillery revetments placed evenly around the points, with sandbagged towers and barracks aboveground. Everything else was underground: the main command bunker, two or three other bunkers, cover for the artillerymen, covered walkways for the riflemen. At the first one, two enemy rounds had badly damaged a .105 howitzer in its pit, and a concreted bunker. Fortunately there had been no men around either at the time. We inspected the holes. When we stood on the parapet with Truong and looked off over the fields that belonged to the Montagnard village behind us, the wooded mountains—faceless and revealing absolutely nothing—began half a mile away from the post. The roly-poly, merry-looking young major who commanded the firebase told Truong that he had the gun spotted and knew where it was, but had not fired on it because of

Truong's orders not to. An aide translated for us. Truong told the major that if they fired on him again, he had his, Truong's, personal permission to fire back and to fire for effect.

The merry, chubby-faced major then took us down into his command bunker for what I was to learn was a standard procedure on these inspection trips. A detailed, point-by-point briefing of everything that had been happening in his area. He showed Truong where the gun was on his big wall map, while we sat in rows of chairs placed like seats in a classroom. The gun had only been moved into the area recently, he explained. This indicated that a great deal of road work had been done on the trails, to get a gun of that size in. Several of his Montagnard villagers had gone over the line into the enemy territory to scout for him, and reported that the North Viets were building concrete culverts wide enough for a one-lane road all along the trails in the area. They were using impressed Montagnards from villages farther back in the hills as a labor force. This was strictly against the cease-fire agreement, Truong turned and said to me in English suddenly. The major added in Vietnamese, which was translated that there was very little that could be done about it, since the American airplanes had been withdrawn. Truong turned his head with its handsome face and liquid eyes and looked at General Hiestand, saying nothing. Hiestand could only smile and spread his hands.

In the rest of the Ranger outposts it was much the same. At the second one a young Ranger lieutenant flubbed up badly on some questions Truong put to him, and got a dressing-down. But there were no screams, no yells, no slaps in the face, no arrests.

Truong put his arm around the embarrassed young officer, and walked off alone with him and talked to him for five or six minutes very gently. Then he patted him on the shoulder, took his salute, and came back to the group. Still unsmiling. And looking almost younger than the lieutenant.

At the divisional headquarters in Quang Ngai lunch was a bowl of "Chinese soup." Truong had little interest in food when he was working. I learned from Hiestand's young American aide that the consultation was about Sa Huynh. Sa Huynh was one of the big fights I had heard about back in Saigon when I first arrived. At the time of the cease-fire the Communists had made a drive to the sea there, and were subsequently thrown out by the South Viets—after the cease-fire. The Communists hollered foul. The story had made the papers for several days. Until something newer came along. The drive had failed, but now they were increasing the pressure on the area, and Truong had come down to make sure there wouldn't be any giving of ground.

Because, strategically, it was a very good move for the North Viets. Their protective mountains came right down to the sea there, giving them supply routes and cover. The area was just at the border between I Corps and II Corps, making liaison between the corps difficult. And if they could take it, they would have a supply port on the sea, as well as permanently cutting Route I between the two Military Regions. It was only a very few minutes after we left Quang Ngai that we flew over My Lai.

General Hiestand tapped me on the shoulder and said into the intercom, "That's My Lai 4, down there." General Truong, who was sitting in front of us and had heard, turned his head around, then motioned to the pilot to circle. Then he made a gesture with his hand to go down a little lower.

I had had no idea it was so near the sea. I had had the mental picture of its being inland somewhere, in a densely jungled area, with lots and lots of paddy fields around it. Actually, it was in the salt flats area. Very little of the land around it was tilled. Most of it was scrub, or bare. Directly below us was an arm of sea water, beyond which was a very thin spit of land and then the sea. The village was on the inland side of the arm of water, on a tertiary road. We were over an area of long, tortuous inlets and sand islands, off of which ran the arm of water that passed the village. "There's My Lai 2, and My Lai 1, and My Lai 3, off over there," Hiestand said. General Truong was looking down from the command seat. He twisted his head around, and looked straight in my eyes. "Very bad, you know," he said into his mike in good English. "Very sad. That is not the way to win the people." I shook my head. "Green troops," Hiestand said over the intercom. "Green troops."

There was really very little to see. The houses clustered in some trees, beside the third-class road. Tin roofs winked up at us. It had been rebuilt, of course. I stole a look around, and saw that everybody was looking at it with the same irresistible horrified awe that I was. Even the pilot was staring down as we circled. My Lai 4. There it was. It would go down into American history as a term synonymous with bloody massacre done by Americans. And Calley and Medina, and Meadlo, and Oliver, and Lee, and the others of Charlie Company would go down with it. Everybody in the helicopter was silent and seemed embarrassed. "You want to see more?" Truong said into his mike. I pushed my thumb button and said, "No." "Then we will go on," Truong said courteously.

An Hai was only about three miles from there, on the same series of tortuous inlets. We came in low, dropping over a fishing village built at the mouth of the main inlet, a double row of fishing sampans in the water. The post was built on top of a bare, red-earth knoll behind the village. Low over it, the prop wash of the copter beginning to swish the grass stalks, I could see it was much less strongly built than the Border Ranger outposts in enemy territory. A single line of open trench circled the hill. Inside it four or five deep holes were dug, and ordinary wood and tin roofs constructed over them. One of these had received a direct hit lately, the mortar round passing through the roof and exploding below it. With a hit like that the sloping protective hole became its own opposite, a veritable deathtrap. I wouldn't have liked to be in it. The round helicopter pad we dropped onto was of crushed stone the size of a double fist.

A squad and a half of ARVN troops had already come in to reinforce the local RF soldiers who manned the post. The ARVN lieutenant took us to inspect the damage. Another round had hit on the lip of the hole. Others had landed outside the line of trench. The post had been hit by a total of twelve rounds in a space of three or four minutes. There had been three men under the direct hit. One had survived with minor injuries, but his eardrums had been burst by the concussion. The two bodies had not yet been removed, and lay under ponchos, their splayed feet making mournful little hills under the fabric in that way dead feet do.

The families would be coming for the bodies, the lieutenant said. And took us down into one of the roofed-over holes for the briefing. On a map of the area he showed the dispositions of ARVN troops who had been sent out to search for the guerrilla group, and the pattern in which others had been sent in the hope of cutting them off. But they probably would not catch them. Truong walked to the map and in his serious, unsmiling, intent way talked to the lieutenant for several minutes. Then suddenly he turned his head and looked straight at me in that direct way he had and said, "You understand two men, two Vietnamese, were killed here last night, this morning." I nodded that I did. "It is not just a problem in mathematics," Truong said. At a signal the lieutenant led us outside for a traditional inspection of the rest of the post. From the parapet we looked off across the dull salt flats and glinting inlets, with clumps of trees here and there on the land, toward where the mortar rounds had come from. I whispered to General Hiestand's young aide, "If there're VC down there, what's to keep them from hitting us right now?" The tall blond boy smiled. "Nothing. If they saw it was a general's helicopter that landed, they would probably try. If they're still there." In a few minutes we were back on board the chopper, whose rotors were already running, and were lifting off. We had an hour's ride ahead of us to Da Nang, and it would be after five o'clock when we arrived. During the ride the slight, slender Truong spoke only once. Some directional comment to the pilot.

When we had landed, Hiestand's aide told me Truong had an official function to go to. Some bigwig up from Saigon. But usually he only put in an appearance, and stayed the required number of minutes and left. Probably he would go back to his office and work late. "One of you writers ought to write his biography or a book about him," the young aide said admiringly. "He's really something a little special." I agreed with him. "If it wasn't for politics, he'd probably be in command of the whole shmeer," the blond boy said.

Dak Pek or not Dak Pek

Mike Healy's call came in for me the next morning. For a while they had trouble finding me, since I was out with Vo exploring the town and the refugee camps outside. Then the Da Nang military operator had a hard time getting Pleiku back. By the time Mike came on the phone, I was a great deal like a man sitting on a fiery hot skillet over a fire.

It was on for Dak Pek, the irrepressible Irishman's voice told me at once. It seemed to me, he knew and had anticipated how anxious I was about it. A South Viet resupply safari was on for tomorrow morning, Mike bellowed into the phone at my ear. And he and Charlie Black had arranged for Charlie and me to go along with them in Mike's command copter. Mike could not go himself, unfortunately. But his U-21 would pick me up at Non Nuoc at two-thirty that afternoon.

The butterflies I had had in my stomach before—about going to Dak Pek—began again even before I had hung up the phone. There wasn't too much time to get packed, have some lunch, get Vo off back to Saigon, and get myself out to Non Nuoc airport to meet the U-21. And as I occupied myself with all of that, the butterflies did not abate.

Coming back to Pleiku was strangely like coming home. The two handsome young pilots with their movie-star haircuts grinned and mock-saluted me and shook hands warmly. The interior of the little U-21 was familiar. When we came down over Pleiku, I remembered the long red-dirt plateau, and Route 14 winding through the Rock Pile pass toward Kontum, and the dusty bristling ant-fortress of the town. The white statue of the Virgin was still on its spit in the lake. Pleiku was the first place I had come in Vietnam outside Saigon and its nest of rumor, when still green as Illinois corn about everything, and Mike Healy and his people were the first people I had met. Now after ten days away and almost three weeks in the country, Pleiku was the first place in Vietnam I had had the opportunity to return to.

Healy's tough, cocky, burr-headed secretary, a young major, met me at the airstrip with one of the cars, chortling happily over the upcoming Dak Pek escapade, and drove me to the SRAC headquarters building. I spent an hour hanging around Charlie Black's office, looking at maps. Black's broad, beat-up face was beaming delightedly. Then I walked back to the quarters area through the immaculate green fortifications. There and on the way, I met at least three senior officers who shook hands warmly, but shook their heads over Dak Pek. None of them thought it was a good idea. None of them would have gone themselves. They had only heard about it unofficially, of course. Officially, they had not heard a word. In my same little room I unpacked again.

Then, only a few minutes after five-thirty and quitting time, Charlie Black came stomping in, his broken face a lowering black cloud. The resupply safari had been postponed. By the South Viets. And it had been postponed indefinitely. There was no telling when it would go, now.

That night after dinner Healy and Black and I sat around Healy's quarters glumly, everybody trying hard to hide his disappointment. There was no point in my staying on in Pleiku, Healy reasoned. I wanted to get on down into the Delta. They had nothing more to show me here. Better I should go back to Saigon tomorrow. He would fly me down tomorrow morning. Meantime, he and Charlie would keep trying to get the resupply mission moving. If anything new came up, he would call me in Saigon at the hotel. Or get me through General Weyand's office. Or call me down in the Delta, if I was there. I reluctantly agreed. But for God's sake, I shouldn't mention anything to General Weyand about it if I saw him, Mike added as we shook hands and I went off to bed.

The Big City

Saigon had seemed a scrawny, barely livable, hick city when I first arrived, after Paris. Not any more. After Pleiku, Kontum, Hue, and Da Nang, it was a sophisticated metropolis. Lights, restaurants, non-military traffic, parties. I felt positively glad to be back. I was so glad I felt like doing something extravagant. I settled for a great "Chinese" lunch with a couple of non-*Times* newsmen, at the big Chinese restaurant off Tu-Do Street. I was still disappointed about Dak Pek. But, finally, I had given up on Dak Pek.

The newsmen were no longer talking about Kontum, since the fighting had slacked off in the North. They were gossiping about two new developments, both in the Delta.

In My Tho in Dinh Tuong Province a VC group had thrown hand grenades into a Buddhist church full of worshippers on a fete day, killing and wounding a large number. Being so near, this greatly upset the people in Saigon.

And in the Seven Mountains area near the Cambodian border in the northwest, new fighting had broken out at Tri Ton and Tinh Bien, and near Hong Ngu farther north. Apparently the North Viets were shifting their pressure from Kontum to the northern Delta.

Saigon had changed in my absence. The National Police Force, for example, that group of happy gunslingers most noted for their corruption and their hard-line torturing of political prisoners, was much more in evidence. You used to see a few of them. Now they were all over, swaggering around the streets in their distinctive uniforms with their pistols slung low on their hips cowboy-style, their faces arch and narrow with an animal vanity, and contempt.

The American military had all but disappeared. There never had been many in Saigon, not since I arrived. But with X+6o Day less than two weeks away now, many had left already and many more were going out every day. There was a sense of the final, last-ditch closing down of a less than wholly successful American experiment in foreign intervention.

A new phenomenon had replaced the military. Since I left Saigon for the North, there had been an enormous influx of American civilians. It was immediately noticeable in the streets. Because these civilians had brought their families with them. And they were everywhere. In the shops and bazaars, the restaurants and bars. You could not cross Tu-Do Street without sidestepping groups of them traveling in fives or sixes.

My newsmen friends told me the civilians were coming in under the new Military Attaché's Office. They were under contract to handle supplies and maintenance of military equipment. The men were hard-faced, hard-muscled, sunburned, and laconic. The wives were talkative, fat-breasted, hard-drinking, with whiskey voices and no waistline to speak of and deep-lined, ungentle faces. The children seemed to be mostly teen-aged girls, gum-chewing, dull-looking, adenoidal, who chewed and chewed and seemed neither surprised nor dismayed nor excited by what they were seeing of another world. Comparatively speaking, these groups made the American military look like clean, innocent young boys.

I almost felt that I was coming back to a different city. There was no more eleven o'clock curfew. Now the curfew was at midnight. And it no longer seemed to be strictly enforced. All at once, after less than three weeks in the country, I quite suddenly felt like an old-timer—a feeling equally as erroneous as feeling it was a different city. Because it wasn't. And I wasn't.

I spent the afternoon sitting around the Continental terrace talking to the hookers with *Times* correspondent Joe Treaster's wife Barbara, the photographer. Charlie Mohr who first told me about Dak Pek had already gone back to Africa. Henry Kamm had gone to Phnom Penh. Fox Butterfield of the *Times*, whom I had never met, had just returned from the United States. After dinner I went up to my room early, because there was nowhere I wanted to go. I was going to have to do something about getting myself down into the Delta. The only way I knew to do that was to go to Fred Weyand again. I was still depressed about the Dak Pek cancellation in Pleiku.

Pleiku Call

It came in the morning, before I had even gone out. I had been down to breakfast in the hotel garden but had not gone over to the bureau office, because I was up in the air and didn't know what I was going to do, whether to call General Weyand about the Delta or not. What I really wanted to do was get up to Tri Ton in the Seven Mountains area on the Cambodian border where the new fighting had broken out, but I was pretty sure it would not be possible. When the operator told me it was a military call from Pleiku, excitement began to jump around in my chest again. Then Mike Healy's phone-voice bellow came on the line.

The canceled Dak Pek resupply had been rescheduled for tomorrow. Mike paused and the Irish grin came into his voice. It had taken some finagling, but he had managed to swing it. And this time, he was going to come along himself. He and Black had worked it all out. I hesitated to ask him what had changed his mind. But then he answered me himself. What the hell, he would be leading a pretty regularized, unexciting life from now on. Besides, a lot of his heart's blood, as well as some of his real blood, had soaked into that country up between Kontum and Dak Pek. Tan Canh, Dak To, Ben Het, Dak Seang, Dak Sut. Also, he did not like the idea of me going up there alone with Charlie, without him with me. I was his responsibility. This way, we would take two machines of our own within the South Viet convoy, Healy and me in his command copter, Black in the next best vehicle flying chase ship for us. That way we would not have to depend on some nervous South Viet bird colonel. Would I be able to come? Then he would send the plane for me this afternoon. A car from Tan Son Nhut would pick me up.

I hung up and stood looking around at my room, which seemed to be an entirely different room from the room it had been ten minutes before. Nothing had been moved, nothing had changed, but it seemed a different room. I set about packing my shaving stuff and boots and a second set of clothes. Now that I was definitely going, about half of me wished I wasn't.

Pleiku and the process of getting to Pleiku were almost second nature by now. I had about become a

Pleiku commuter. This time one of the two young pilots grinned knowingly. Going up to Dak Pek tomorrow, was I? he told me. Well, he wished me luck. That night at dinner in Healy's mess another officer was given his Montagnard knife and I sat beside one of the worldlier of Healy's staff colonels, Colonel Kaplan, who shook his head at me. He wouldn't go on that trip tomorrow for anything in God's world, he grinned. It was that same worldly colonel, who was Jewish and came from somewhere in California I think, who after dinner came and got me in Healy's quarters, to come sit in on the poker game they had going in the club room. They had heard I'd been playing some poker over in Da Nang, he smiled, and they figured if I was going to Dak Pek tomorrow, I might as well leave some of my money here with them as give it all to the North Vietnamese. This sally drew a gust of laughter from Healy and Black.

Dollar, Two Buck, Five

Dak Pek seemed to be on the mind of the whole command. Just walking around the area, I had been greeted over and over again by officers and men who did not know me, but who waved, and grinned, and welcomed me back with sly smiles. The same thing was apparent when Colonel Kaplan brought me up to the old, beat-up poker table in the equally dilapidated club room. I was greeted with sardonic smiles by the players, and several comments about my poker in

Da Nang, but there was this curious warmth and excitement emanating from them whenever Dak Pek was mentioned. A suppressed, subterranean current of anticipation ran through the outfit.

The club room wasn't much. Behind us was a six-pocket pool table that also had seen better days, with a cone of light over it that lit up the swirls of tobacco smoke in the air. Right next door was the bar, where the evening's movie was being shown. Every time the door opened between, choruses of whistles, groans and ironic cheers were blown in at us. The scene and the faces were so American that it warmed me.

The game was being banked by Healy's burr-head, cocky young secretary, Major Deke Cuttell. Who was apparently used to winning. And whom, apparently, the others were used to losing to. The minimum take-out was fifty dollars, drawn in chips from Cuttell, a dollar ante, two bucks to open or first bet, five bucks to raise, and after that table stakes—whatever you had in front of you.

Right from the start I began to get good cards and to win big pots. I was tense and keyed up and high over tomorrow and it made it easy for me to concentrate. Besides, I had my fiasco in Da Nang sitting on my shoulder that I wanted to wipe out. They played a lot of stud, seven-card high-low, seven-card high only, seven-card lowball, all games I liked. And they played a lot a game I did not know, in which five cards are dealt facedown as in draw poker, the game opened and bet as in draw, then cards were drawn as in draw, but after that the five cards were arranged and placed facedown and turned up and bet one at a time, as in the five-card stud game called Mississippi Roll'em. It was a game that made for big pots, and I won several of these. In one hand of seven-card high only, I was dealt an ace-queen flush in clubs the first five cards. My friend the colonel, on my left, filled a king-high flush in diamonds (the ace was visible elsewhere on the table), another man filled a straight, and a third made three of a kind. All three of them stayed for twenty dollars. At the end of an hour I was ahead almost two hundred dollars.

There were some revisions of thinking at the table about my poker. Then the luck left me. It passed across the table to Cuttell, and seemed to divide its time between Cuttell and a chunky captain sitting next to him, and I started sitting on my winnings. Getting money out of me that night was going to be like pulling teeth out of a boar hog. As my grandfather used to say. Several men got wiped out and left. Or got tired or disgusted and quit. They were replaced by new fortune hunters. An hour and a half of this, and I felt the luck pass back to me on one particular hand, and began to win again. After a little more than three hours in all, I had won three hundred and forty dollars, and announced I would have to quit because I had somewhere to go tomorrow early.

It was not a huge win. But it was the biggest win at the table that night. And the vindication I was after.

My remark drew an appreciative laugh from the table, and the hangers-on. But then two seats to my left, just beyond the colonel, a freckle-faced, sandy-haired, snub-nosed young boy, who looked like a painting of an American boy by Norman Rockwell except that Rockwell had never painted a face that tough, and who had been losing steadily and silently all evening, looked up and said blandly, "You better hang onto the money. Because it'll cost you that to-morrow for me to get you back from Dak Pek."

That broke up the table. I didn't get it and could only look at him, until beside me my friend Colonel Kaplan explained, "He's the copter pilot who'll be flying Colonel Black's chase ship tomorrow." I could sense the table waiting delightedly to see if I was going to have an answer, so I grinned and said, "If you have to come down for me tomorrow, I'll be glad to give it all to you. Matter of fact," I added, "I think I'll leave it all right here with the colonel, to give you an added incentive to make sure I get back."

This was successful enough to draw a laugh, and some vocal applause, and when I stood up, there was a chorus of well-wishing and good-lucking for me for tomorrow. I just stood and looked at them. Just for something as simple-minded as that, they were vot-ing me into their arrogant corporation, letting me inside, me a man old enough to be father to most of them, accepting me if not as an equal, at least as an apprentice. I could only stand and look at them. Be-side me, my friend the wise Jewish colonel turned his head far enough so that none of them could see his off eye, and gave me a cognizant, worldly wink. Don't tip it, his eye said. I winked back at him. And waved at the table, and stepped back to put away my winnings. Colonel Kaplan dropped out and left with me, two new men immediately taking our seats. The colonel walked me down the long porch to my room. Healy and Black had already gone to bed. At my door he shook hands and wished me luck tomorrow, and then shook his head and grinned.

Dak Pek

The assembly area was a big dusty field on the outskirts of Pleiku somewhere in the Viet command center. We got there early in Healy's car. Our two unarmed helicopters came in and landed in a cloud of dust fifteen minutes later. There was one Viet command copter armed with .50 calibers on the ground. But that was all. Then, finally, the Vietnamese began to arrive.

The field where we were assembling was an official departure point. A frame dispatcher's office sat just beside the gate in the field. Behind it was strung out a line of lean-to sheds for supplies that were to be picked up and airlifted. At the far end of them, squatting or standing patiently in the shade of the last shed, was a group of about twenty Montagnards, in their grubby, highly colored, gypsy-looking outfits.

I asked Charlie Black what they were doing there. Black looked at them as if his mind was far away on something else, then shrugged. Waiting for a ride, he said. Probably they had relatives serving at Dak Pek, or else they were from Dak Pek and had been down here visiting. They had heard a resupply was going up and had come to beg a ride. They probably had been there two or three days, waiting. Before, when our American troops were here, there had been lots of rides. Now it was more difficult. And it was the only way they could travel in VC country. You would find them waiting patiently at every airport and heliport in the Highlands.

The first Vietnamese to arrive were two truckloads of about twenty Montagnard Rangers each, all of them nattily dressed out in their red berets and scarves and starched combat camouflage fatigues, and carrying light packs and rifles. The two captains reported formally to Healy. Healy took their salutes, then gave Charlie Black a dark look. What the hell was going on, Charlie? he wanted to know. This looked like they were sending up a relief force. Black could only shrug and look perturbed. Nobody had told him about it. Healy looked at his watch and began to fidget. Still no Viet command officers.

Another twenty minutes passed. Then two trucks loaded with heavy machineguns and what to me looked like an enormous amount of ammunition, pulled in at the gate and stopped. The ammo was still in its US Quartermaster cases. The red-bereted troopers began to unload the two trucks. Healy began to swear. He was obviously liking what he saw less and less.

Another twenty minutes, and the Viet brass began to arrive. In what appeared to be an endless string of official vehicles. There were two command cars and three jeep loads of them. The last jeep was filled with nothing but full colonels, and a major general in a red beret commanded it.

The big field now looked as if it were the jump-off point of a major military campaign. More jeeps and trucks of administrative and service troops had crowded into the field. Three more Huey command copters dropped down swirling the dust and landed. There must have been three hundred people in the big field.

The little major general hopped out and bounced over to Healy, who towered a foot and a half over him. A ritual, long-winded round of handshaking between all the officers on both sides was begun. Then the Viet general went off to inspect his operation.

Healy had been in high humor back at his quarters, but now his face was getting blacker and blacker. He and Colonel Black went into an angry, muttered conference. Then Healy went off to talk to a Viet major he'd been given as an interpreter.

It was clear enough what had happened. Healy had expected to ride along on a normal resupply mission. The Viet general—who, naturally, would not be going —had turned it into a big deal, turning the normal resupply into a much bigger resupply plus a personnel relief operation, in honor of the departing American advisor. A personnel relief which, I learned from Black who had come back beside me, had been militarily long overdue. So the Viet general gained points for two major events—a relief mission which should already have been done some time back anyway, and a farewell celebration for Healy which was valueless and could even be dangerous, if he went. Black of course had known nothing about it, and had not been told. Maybe they wanted to surprise us, he said bitterly.

And now Healy would have to go, I said. He had no way out.

No. He didn't have to go, Black told me. He could just tell the bastards he'd changed his mind. Black had seen him do it. "He doesn't give a damn," Black

164

said. "That's how he can get things done. He really doesn't give a damn."

In front of us, Healy was now talking away with the Viet general as if he had never had a gloomy thought in his life. Back at his quarters, he had jammed his precious old green beret in his fatigue pants side pocket, saying he would like to wear it when he inspected Dak Pek, although it was illegal. Now, before the red-bereted Viet officers, he pulled it out suddenly, and pulled off his green baseball fatigue cap and with a grin put on the beret. He probably could not have done anything that would have pleased the Vietnamese more, and he knew it.

But when he came back to us, he was no longer smiling. The whole thing was a foul-up, he told us immediately. Like all these major operations, it was beginning to show unmistakable signs of turning into a fiasco. As always, the more people that got involved in an operation, the more error there was. The Viets were planning on taking forty-five replacement personnel up to Dak Pek. They were taking four Hueys and four of the big Chinook "hooks." With our two, that made ten helicopters in the air. Not even the most peace-minded North Viet gunner in the world could resist a target like that. An air convoy that big could not help but draw fire, and we would be sitting in the middle of it. He was beginning to not like it at all. Did I still want to go? I quickly said I didn't want to go if it was against his better judgment. Healy just nodded, and looked at his watch again. Not only that, the hooks had not even left their field yet. They would have to fly over here, maneuver themselves down, get themselves loaded—it would be at least an hour before they could go. So what we were going to do was to go ahead. We would stop at the airport in Kontum and wait for the rest of the convoy there. He had already informed the Ranger general, so we could get going.

Beside me, Charlie Black nodded and then pulled out his own green beret and put it on. At the helicopters we split, after shaking hands, Healy and I to ours, Black to the chase ship. When I looked up at the bubble nose of the chase ship, the pilot from last night waved and mock-saluted me. I mock-saluted back.

In the helicopter Healy was pensive and quiet. After we were in the air, he pushed his mike button once, and said he would decide whether to abort the trip when we got to Kontum. Off to our right down the shallow valley, far below us one of the four hooks was just getting into the air. When I leaned out a little and looked up, the ship of Black and my poker-playing buddy from last night was riding five hundred or a thousand feet above and behind us.

Decision

Soon the now ancient Rock Pile battlefield was below us on the road on our right. Nothing was as old as an old battlefield when new actions were taking place. Then the remembered tortuous curvings of the river flashed at us. The pilot swung us low over the town to land at the airport on the eastern edge.

I had not landed at Kontum airport before. It was

such a scene of devastation that it shocked me. The biggest part of the battle for Kontum in the 1972 offensive had happened here. Burnt-out trucks and smashed helicopters and airplanes dotted the flat terrain. Just visible in the distance, two bombed-out, rusting Russian tanks squatted. The airport building had taken a lot of fire, and unrepaired shell holes and the pockmarks of small-arms fire gaped in its walls. Its holed tile roof had been patched with tin. The huge carcass of a ruined C-147 had been shoved off the runway against a line of trees, and some Montagnards had set up housekeeping in it. Motionless and silent, they stood or squatted against it and looked at us. Another group, dressed in their finery, waited with limitless patience beside the airport building for the airplane ride that would take them somewhere. In the midst of all this ruin, we had landed out beyond the runway on a blacktop in some grass near some buildings which had been reduced to their foundations, and the thing that shocked me most was that under our feet when we climbed down the ground was one vast carpet of expended M-16 cartridge cases. Such an expenditure of ammunition seemed unbelievable. The firepower it represented was incredible. As far as I could see clearly, in every direction except the airplane runway itself, with only a few small bare patches here and there, this enormous carpet of brass stretched away, a mute but tinkling memorial to the depth and commitment of the fighting that had gone on.

In the middle of this devastated scene, Healy sat down on a half-burnt beam in the sun to wait. Without saying a single word. Every so often he looked at his watch. After a while he pulled a GI pocket knife out and began to cut on a piece of stick, whistling soundlessly through his teeth.

By a sort of tacit common consent, everybody left him strictly alone. The pilots and gunless gunners stood in the shade of their choppers. Charlie Black had immediately come over from his ship, his flat busted face wrinkled with concern, but then did not speak. It was Healy's decision to make, and Healy would have to make it. Nobody would question it. Everyone knew the problem. All of our lives might depend on what he decided. Yet I had the distinct, surprising impression that not one man among us wanted to abandon the mission and go back to Pleiku without having been to Dak Pek.

I was getting to see Healy in action, and I was fascinated. Back in his quarters earlier he had been expansive. At the assembly field he had gotten more and more irritable and fidgety until he was as edgy as a cat. Now he had sunk down into himself until he was in any practicable sense unreachable. Nor was he looking anywhere outside for assistance. The intensity and energy he brought to it were fantastic. He was more like a forest animal sniffing the wind than a man rationalizing. His years of experience and the meticulous Special Forces training had become such a part of his internal being that he sort of smelled out a decision, like a dog after a rabbit. Better than thinking it consciously. After a minute he looked at his watch once more, then up at the still empty sky, and then stood up with a grin, put his pocket knife away, and kicked at the carpet of rolling brass underfoot. We would go ahead by ourselves, on our own, he said. What the hell, they might never get that top-heavy operation off the ground at all. If they did, we would be ahead of them. Anyone who did not want to go, did not have to. We would leave them here, and pick them up on the way back.

No one asked to stay. Quietly the men began to move away, but I saw several grins passed back and forth. It was an eminently satisfactory decision. If the big convoy did draw fire, we would not be in it. And we would be flying ahead of them, not behind them into excited and alerted NVA gunners. At the same time, we could honestly declare that we were with the convoy, and had not gone off to Dak Pek alone on our own against orders. We were just a little ahead, because they were late starting. And, finally, none of us would have to go back to the command in Pleiku without having been to Dak Pek. I for one had been ready to abide wholeheartedly and without regrets by whatever he decided, even if he had decided to abort the trip. Now, I began to wonder if Mike had not had some such idea as this at the bottom of his mind all along. In any case, he had maneuvered himself into . a position ahead of time, to be able to do just exactly what he was doing.

In the helicopter Healy handed me a flak jacket to put on, and then with a grin handed me a second one to sit on. There were other important parts of a man to protect besides just his heart, he said delicately. Then he laughed his wild, Irishman's laugh, and the blue eyes glinted. Decisions made, he was again the high-humored man he had been back in his quarters before we drove off to the assembly point. The flak jacket was uncomfortable to sit on, but I was grateful for it.

In the Air

I had been awed and a little daunted by the magnitude of the operation, back at the assembly point. Now, with just the two helicopters revving up, as the pilots started their motors, it was the kind of quick, clean, intimate, hit-and-run mission I had originally envisioned.

Above Kontum, we climbed in tight spiraling circles. Healy had set 5000 feet as a minimum safety level, which with a ground level of 3000 feet above sea level made an aggregate height of 8000 on the altimeter. Quickly the attitudes of the town and its defenses became visible, readable as on a map; then as quickly faded to a smaller, impersonal conglomeration. Wire defenses, open trenches, and series of bunkers surrounded it to the north and west, running almost as far east as the airfield. Two kilometers north on Route 14 a cluster of bunkers marked the roadblock which was the forward line of the North Viet Army. At home it was easy to talk about the basic kindliness and good intentions of the VC and North Viets. Out here (I realized suddenly, perhaps more than I ever had) in Vietnam, they were the enemy. They would kill you if they could. Especially in a flimsy helicopter above their lines, they were the enemy.

Up here in the upper air, the constant BLAT, BLAT, BLAT of the helicopter motor, loud even through the

big earphone helmets, was comforting, but also dis-
comforting, in that it constantly reminded you it was
all that was keeping you up there. If it stopped, we
would drop like a stone. I pulled out a fresh, small
notebook I had brought along to keep a minute by
minute journal.

At 0923 we crossed the creek line west of the road
that was the VC boundary. Healy looked up and
grinned. "They may be shooting at us down there. But
we're too high for them to hope to hit us." There was
truck traffic on the road, but nothing visible below us.
Healy was sitting far forward in his adjustable command chair watching everything below intently.
There were some antiaircraft positions farther on, he
said absently. They might have a try at us. But they'd
have to be very lucky. 5000 feet was above their range.

Almost immediately we passed Firebase November
on the road. Healy pointed it out. And I remembered
the young lt colonel with the scarred face who had
shipped out the day I arrived, and his friend. The
North Vietnamese apparently had done nothing with
it and it was unmanned and empty.

At 0927 we were crossing the town of Tan Canh.
Tan Canh was what I had heard so much talk about
in Pleiku when I first arrived. There had been a ter-
rific fight there last December, before we lost it, Healy
said. We had lost a lot of good men there. There was
a kind of reverence in his voice as he looked down at
it. We had covered forty kilometers, about twenty
miles, in just four minutes. The first antiaircraft was
just up ahead, Healy said.

Tan Canh was certainly not unmanned. It was full
of truck traffic, and was in process of being built up
and fortified, and Healy began to curse quietly,

tensely, as he pointed out the new ground positions and firebases. All this was strictly against the rules of the cease-fire. He dragged out a baby-sized notebook and began jotting notes. Might as well utilize the opportunity. So was this against the cease-fire, he looked up and grinned; but no more—not as much—as what they were doing down there.

There were eight of us in the helicopter. The two pilots, the two gunners (without guns), Healy and I in the command seats, the Viet major of Rangers Healy had been assigned as interpreter, and Cai, Healy's Viet aide. Cai and the Viet major began laughing on their long seat behind the radio console as we crossed Tan Canh, and Healy looked over at them and grinned and then looked at me. They were laughing because Cai had had a helicopter tipped over on him there at Tan Canh, by artillery fire. Colonel Vann— the famous John Paul Vann—had pulled it off him under fire.

In spite of his occasional grins Healy's geared-up intentness did not flag. He watched everything, both on the ground and in the air, moving his eyes continually. When we crossed the known antiaircraft positions, Healy pointed them out to me but I couldn't see them. I asked if they fired time fuses. Time fuses exploded in the air at a given height, whereas contact fuses had to hit something. They used both, Healy said. But their effective range was only around 3000 ft. But they'd been known to hit helicopters higher. We'd be able to see time fuses. But we were too high to see flashes or smoke on the ground, so it was impossible to tell if they were firing contact fuses at us. If they were firing contact fuses, the only way we would know it was if one hit us. Then we'd know. He gave me a tight, tough, almost mean, grin. It was possible to survive a hit, one hit, he added. Below us at about 4000 ft, some smoke flowers blossomed suddenly. Healy pointed to them. They were probably 37 mm's, which had an effective range of about 4500 ft. Luckily, the 23 mm's didn't seem to be firing.

At 0935 (my notes said) we passed Ben Het. Ben Het was a Border Ranger post that in 1969, 1970–71, had withstood repeated NVA attacks under very heavy fire. Part of that time Healy had commanded it. In 1969 the South Viets were under siege there for 61 days straight at Christmas time. Right now the ICCS was supposed to be in there, checking on whether the North Viets were allowing free access to supply it. Healy grinned sardonically. Looking down on it from 5000 ft, it did not look big enough or well enough situated to have sustained the kind of fire attacks it had survived. It was almost entirely surrounded by antiaircraft positions, Healy said, as was Dak Pek. If they weren't firing contact fuses at us right now, it was only because the ICCS was in there at this very moment. We had not spotted any ICCS copters.

By 0939 we had passed Dak Seang, and by 0941 were coming up on Dak Pek. The Viet major began calling it on radio. But had trouble with his head set. Healy gave him his. I gave Healy mine.

0946. (my notes said). Can see the camp. No fire coming up. Viet major in contact by radio. Speaking to camp commander.

The camp was a pretty awesome major installation. At least six hills had been heavily fortified, terraced with different levels of wire and obstacles. It was like looking at a two-color terrain contour map. Four of the hills had been connected into one large single post. Two others were large, outlying autonomous posts. Out beyond these were smaller observation posts and firebases.

0949. (my notes said). Radio says situation cool at camp. Can land. Do we want airstrip or pad? Will give us smoke.

0950. Turning hard in and down. Yellow smoke grenade on pad. Tight circle straight down.

But that did not even begin to describe it. If I had thought the climbing circles tight at Kontum, it had been a rank novice's opinion. Now we seemed to be turning on a half dollar. The helicopter was spiraling down within its own overall length. We had flown up straight over the camp at 5500 ft to avoid fire, and now Healy's pilot was taking us absolutely straight down around a perpendicular axis. My head filled with blood, and vertigo rushed up at me from my chest, making me want to shut my eyes. From the command seat Healy grinned and winked at me. I managed to wink back. Closer down, I could see that almost everything was bunkered and sandbagged and underground, with connecting trenches, clusters of mortar pits and sunken artillery revetments, all well kept. Only shacks and flimsy sheds and one or two main buildings were aboveground.

0953. My notes said, simply, "Down."

Down

The camp commander was a Viet major. He and his staff, all grinning hugely, were waiting for us at the pad, which was well inside the main wire of the main camp. There had not been a "white" man at Dak Pek in three to four months. When they saw the two green berets jump down out of the two helicopters, they shouted a cheer. I looked at Healy, who blushed and gave me a wink.

The Viet major was a slim, good-looking, and sophisticated-looking young guy with highly intelligent eyes. He looked much too bright to be the field commander out here at Dak Pek in the boon docks (and later Healy told me he had only been there a month, having been given the assignment as a punishment for political statements he had made). He had apparently been around, because he spoke very good English, and gave his briefing in English for the American advisors.

As I had learned, these briefings were almost a religious ritual at the Ranger outposts. The map on the wall, the blackboard, the chairs arranged like a classroom. An inheritance from the Americans. That would go on, long after they had left. Healy had not particularly meant to have a briefing, but he settled in and participated respectfully. He asked pertinent questions.

He was, the Viet major said, surrounded by three platoons of NVA and one reinforced company of VC. Refugees coming in reported the VC were using 500 Montagnards to widen the trail from their positions out to Route 14 and make it into a main supply road. We all knew what that meant, he smiled. Artillery. In the south the VC were repairing and rebuilding Route 14. A recon patrol of his to the south showed a big North Viet build-up all around the area. The enemy main supply route south bypassed the Dak Pek camp, a long hard detour. Naturally, the NVA and VC would like to remove it. He expected them to try at any time. On the other hand, his forces were in very high morale. Yesterday three Montagnards who had escaped the VC work gangs gave a talk to the camp Montagnards about what life was like under the VC. He had found, the major said, that the best propaganda of all was simply to let the escapees tell the truth to the Montagnards in the camp. He was sweet and eager in his English, the major, and very proud of the way he spoke it.

He analyzed his troop organization for us. He had one Reconnaissance Company, of which one recon platoon remained constantly in the camp, with the other three periodically patrolling. And he had the 88th Border Ranger Battalion. The Ranger Battalion broke down into 78 Vietnamese, officers and non-coms, and 355 Montagnards. With ranks running from private up to captain. He seemed proud of that, the major. He even broke down the Montagnards for us, by tribal unit. He had:

181 Tem
56 Halang
18 Rhadé
47 Sedang
46 Jarai
7 Bahnar
—————
355

With these 355 troopers were 326 Montagnard families, living in the camp. Each family averaged five persons, man, women, and children. A total of 1630 Montagnards in the camp.

Since he had been here, he had been teaching the women to shoot and to handle and load, both the carbine and M-16, and to carry artillery ammunition during VC attacks. There had been two light attacks since his investiture, and the women had been a big help in repulsing them.

If he was bitter or bereaved about his punishment assignment, the major certainly didn't show it.

As we went out with him to follow him through a camp inspection, Healy gave me one quick burning, poignant look that I felt all the way down to the soles of my boots.

I think the whole of the main four-hill installation must have been easily a half a mile across. I do not think I saw more than four trees within it. Tall, spindly, telephone-pole-type creatures, with only a few branches of foliage up near the top. The rest was bare dirt. Bare dirt, and sandbags. Most of the shacks and sheds I had seen from the air were Montagnard dwelling places, and were constructed as semibunkers. Holes in the ground with sandbagged walls aboveground covered with cloth or tin or wood and

roofed with pieces of tent or corrugated tin or plat-
forms of rough boards. The Montagnards were great
at making do with little. But it must have been hell
during the rainy season. In the hot sun of the dry
season it was blazing hot on the ground without
cover, but the mountain air was fresh, unlike the low-
lands around Hue and Da Nang. The dwelling holes
generally followed the contour of the terraces, close
to the open trenches, where the men—and women,
now—could leap out into them armed and ready to
fight.

Around our party as we moved, the daily life of the
camp went ahead. Barefooted Yard soldiers squatted
by their holes whittling wooden tools. Long-haired
Yard women in their dust-grimed hand-woven finery
pounded grain in wooden mortars or carried water in
earthen jars, or swung the big wicker shields they
used for winnowing. Wood was the fuel for all the
cooking fires. The men hunted, the major said, but as
the available game in the forest was used up, they
had to keep going farther and farther out. Delicately,
he asked Healy about the resupply mission. Healy
explained to him about our coming ahead of it.

From the top of the highest hill of the main camp,
the situation was easy to read. The camp sprawled
across most of the narrow valley, guarding Highway
14 that ran down it. Almost fully encircling it, high
forested hills loomed above it, and would have made
great artillery positions from which to pound the
camp to dust. Fortunately the jungle made them difficult of access. So far the North Viets had not wanted
to expand the men, matériel, and effort to utilize
them. To the south, and to the west where most of the
attacks came from, a mile or so of flat land stretched

to the blank-faced forested hills, and was a tangle of downed timber. Almost everything had been cut down, blown down by fire, or sawed off to make fields of fire and observation, and to make it hard for the enemy to move. Parts of it looked as if they had burned.

From the high point looking all around, you could see that it was a veritable deathtrap, given sufficient men and firepower of the enemy. But it was also an internal deathtrap, too. Despite all the homeliness of the daily camp life. At least five times as we passed from one area to another, the major had to stop and deactivate electrically operated claymore mines before we could pass through gates in the internal wire tangle to the next area. It was all arranged, and they were prepared, to sell the place a foot at a time.

From the western parapet where we stood and looked off at the hills from which attacks usually came, while Montagnard women cooked all around us, three human skeletons were visible in the scramble of barbed wire down the forward slope. The major apologized for them. They were VC left over from a heavy attack in January. But he could not get to them safely to bury them because they were in a mine field there were no charts for.

As we all walked back down, the lithe little major moved up beside me, smiling. He had read *Tant qu'il y aura des hommes,* he said, and thought it was a great soldier's book. How did I like their little establishment? I said I thought it was remarkable, and then risked a word I wasn't sure would be understood. "It's beautiful," I said. Beautiful? he said; yes, perhaps it was beautiful. He would be glad to arrange for me to stay with them a week or so if I wanted, he said with a grin. I grinned back at him and said I'd better stick with General Healy. He nodded, grinning more. They had only had two light feeling attacks and two fairly heavy mortarings, since the January cease-fire. I nodded and just winked at him. General Healy was a great soldier, he said. He was known to all the Montagnards. He loved these people, and they loved him. They were delighted a general would come to say good-by to them.

Down at the helicopter we said good-by, and went through all the handshaking ritual. Healy and the major embraced each other.

As we strapped ourselves in, Mike let out a sigh and grinned. Now all we had left to do was to get out of this place, and get back to home base with a whole skin. I asked what was to stop the VC from dropping some mortar rounds in on us while we were downed here, and he pondered a moment. Nothing at all, he said. If they had had a crew in close enough, they probably would have. We had probably just surprised them. Did I know, he had fought alongside that little major. Way back when he was still a boy lieutenant. He had all the makings of a great soldier. It was tough, hard to leave them all up here in this hellhole.

I checked my safety-belt fastening, and suddenly remembered a nursery rhyme I had used to say as a baby.

> Ladybug, ladybug, fly away home
> Your house is on fire
> And your children will burn.

Fly Home

1045. Off the ground and up and circling tight to climb. At the top, in the same way that a tornado cloud does, we widened and relaxed the circle a little to let me take photos. 1048, off for home. That was the note I made, and it sounded good in my ear as I wrote it. Healy's combative tension and his geared-up sensory response had come back over him the second we lifted off, and he watched everything with the intentness and mental concentration of a hunting hawk. He kept repeatedly looking up forward to check the pilots, and back rearward to check the gunless gunners.

Over Dak Seang he looked down at it woodenly. Like a man who is probably really seeing something for the last time in his life, and saying good-by. All he said was, "Dak Seang took a beating." Then he looked up and pressed his mike button and gave me a half-shy, half-aggressive laugh, and began to tell me the tale of how he had been shot down there in 1970. From fifteen feet up. Fortunately it hadn't been higher. But if they'd been higher the mortar round mightn't have got them. The helicopter had lit on its side, but the fuel tanks didn't ignite. The fall had sprained his back, but Cai and the others had got him out and back inside the walls. Another copter had picked them up an hour or so later.

Farther down he pointed out what was called

"Rocket Ridge" to me, and showed me how it dominated Tan Canh and the Dak To area. The North Viets had come in from the west and taken Rocket Ridge as a base. The ridge itself ran almost all the way down to Kontum. We had never really cleared it or taken it back, and he pointed out the road they'd built along its flank, which ran down to the flats along Route 14. In 1972 they had "poured down" from there to attack Kontum from the west.

At 1103 I noticed suddenly that the pilot was pulling at his right leg with his hand, making a terrible face. For a quick flash my heart bounded and I thought he had been hit by something, just as Healy asked sharply, *"What's the matter?"* The pilot's voice came on to say it was nothing, as he turned and grinned back at us. He'd gotten a cramp in his leg, was all. Behind us Cai and the Viet major began to laugh, then Healy joined them, then I did.

We were below Tan Canh now, and below the known antiaircraft positions, and Healy began to relax a little. Off to the west on our right, not far below the southern end of the long Rocket Ridge, he pointed out Polei Kleng, an old Special Forces camp which had fallen when Ben Het was hit. He had worked out of there many a time, he said. Then he said again what I had already heard him and so many other US officers say in Vietnam, and would hear a number of times again: I'd like to come back here someday, and see how everything worked out.

Five minutes later we passed the creek line that marked the NVA line, then Kontum, miles away to the east on our left. We were back inside. At 1116. Grinning, Healy pressed his mike button and told the pilot to stay up high. He didn't want some VC clown ramming around down there in the brush to hit us with a hand-held SA-7, now. At 1122 Pleiku came in sight. At 1127 we flew over the well-remembered statue of the Virgin on her spit out in the lake. A minute later at 1128 we set down at the pad behind the SRAC headquarters building. I hoped the Virgin was smiling on her pedestal, because I sure as hell was. We had been gone just about two hours and twenty-eight minutes. But it seemed like a year.

At the Compound

Grinning, Healy went in to report our return to his Viet counterpart the II Corps commander, who apparently had advised him against the trip, and then we drove down to his quarters. There was a mild celebration in Healy's quarters. Most of the staff stopped in for a jubilant beer, and to congratulate Healy and Black—and me—on the success of the trip. I tried to stay out of the way as much as possible, not having done anything except sit there beside Healy during the trip. Besides, it was rather a sad occasion for me, because I was leaving that afternoon for Saigon again. Healy was flying back down for more dental appointments, and I was going with him. I had gotten to like enormously the men of Healy's command, and I would not be seeing them again.

And as well, in a way I seemed to already know that Dak Pek was the high point of my time in Vietnam. The apex on the graph of the initial incursion. After

which everything else must necessarily be diminu-
tion, downhill, shading off, to inevitable departure.
There was this inescapable feeling that after I left
Pleiku this time, I was beginning the leg out.

At one point young Major Deke Cuttell said to me,
with a kind of half-guilty grin I did not fully understand the reason for, "You really took your life in your
hands. I hope you were nodding and praying." Behind
him Col Joe Vivaldi, the chief of staff, a husky blocky
man with a boxer's nose, said, "Well, we were all
keeping our fingers crossed. *And* our legs." This was
said with his customary wry smile, but his gaze was
a little wondering. My poker friend Colonel Kaplan
only looked at me and grinned and shook his head.
Across the room, Mike Healy in his customary arm-
chair, who had heard Joe Vivaldi, kicked his feet off
the floor, his blue eyes flashing, and hollered, "You
didn't know how dangerous you were living, baby!"
and laughed. I could only grin. "Maybe," I said. "But
last night when I went to bed I sure knew it." They all
laughed. So I told him I had taken the occasion last
night to write a letter to my wife, and he roared.
"Come on," he bellowed. "Let's get something to eat.
I'm starved."

Why did he really think they hadn't fired on us today? I asked. He shook his head. Maybe they had. Yes,
but they hadn't gone all out for us, I said, or we'd have
seen some time fuses exploding. Healy nodded, and
pondered a moment. Who knew? he said. The idea
was to go early enough so they would still be sleepy
and feeling lazy. "Who knows? Maybe they were just
feeling in a good mood today."

For some reason this gave me a strangely chilly
feeling. That it could depend on just that.

Later, we were to get a report that the relief and resupply had in fact not gone that day, but had gone several days later. They had taken heavy fire at two different places, and one of the big hooks had been hit. It had managed to land at Dak Pek but would not be able to return until repaired. One report had it that two men were killed and four wounded. Another had it only that two men had been wounded.

The Difficulty of Saying Good-by and Thank You

Healy's dental appointments in Saigon would keep him occupied the better part of the two days he was staying, and when he was not occupied with them, he had conferences and meetings to attend right on into the night up to bedtime. And I had to start bending my time to getting myself somehow down into the Delta, preferably up in the north of it around Tri Ton and Hong Ngu, if possible. So there was not much chance of our meeting up again in Saigon after we got there.

Over and over, some individual member of Healy's staff when alone with me would say, in a kind of straining effort to convince me, something like, "You don't know. He just doesn't do things for people very often, like this. I don't know what you told him, but you sure sold him." I didn't know why they felt they had to convince me, I didn't need convincing.

After crossing the creek line and passing Kontum, before we got to Pleiku, I had talked to Healy about my hopes and my trouble about getting down into the Delta. How I hated to bother General Weyand with my small affairs. Healy had said there was no question about it. I should call General Weyand and ask him for help. At the same time, he thought he knew a way maybe he could help me. He would call George D. Jacobson at the Embassy when he got to Saigon. Jacobson was a former Army colonel, who had retired to stay and work in Vietnam as had John Paul Vann. Jacobson was now with CORDS, the civil operations side, and knew just about everything about the Delta.

We talked about the same thing again in the little U-21 on the flight down to Saigon. Healy said he would call me at the hotel as soon as he had spoken with Jacobson, when he got in to a phone.

At the airport he insisted on dropping me off at the hotel on his way to the Army hospital. As we drove through the wild, dusty Honda traffic into town, I kept looking out the window, trying to think of some brilliant, cocky, witty way of telling him how much I appreciated all he had done for me. Like most arrogant, humorous men, he appreciated humorous arrogance in others.

When the car stopped in front of the Continental Palace and I got out, I turned back to the interior of the car and stuck out my hand. "Good-by," I said. "Thank you."

Healy took the hand. "Forget it," he said. "You're welcome."

White Thighs

Maurice Girodias's Olympia Press once published a porno novel called *White Thighs,* about some cat who hired a fat Swedish masseuse to dominate him, which I bought and read without too much interest. It wasn't much of a book, though it would be a collector's item today, and was stolen from me by the Negro maid in a midtown New York hotel, but its title makes a perfect description of the general impression and effect the American female new arrivals had made on Saigon.

It might not have been so bad if they had not all been wearing "hot-pants" shorts all the time. But all of them had come prepared for the tropical weather. And the daughters' legs appeared to be no better than the mothers'. It was amazing they did not get sunburned. I saw one or two cases of the backs of knees burned a bright painful pink, but in general their legs stayed as white as the milk and other dairy products they were addicted to. Amongst the slender Viet women in their black pajama pants and *ao-dai* you could see those fat white legs for blocks.

I was suddenly reminded of a summer I had spent in America a couple of years back. Part on Long Island, part in Pennsylvania. In both places, after Europe, the enormity of the American thigh had the same effect on my eyes as in Saigon. In that case the thighs were tanned, but it didn't make any difference.

They were just white thighs that had been tanned. To
see a slim, long-muscled female leg in all the shorts
on the street, you had to go clear down into the eleven-
and twelve-year-old Lolita class. And every day when
you went to town, you would find them all congregat-
ing in the milk bars and ice cream parlors for their
malts and shakes and splits and sundaes. It was almost as bad a curse as our American style of alcohol-
ism. And I could remember how as a boy I had been
taught almost religiously to drink my quart of milk a
day or some horrible disease like tuberculosis would
soon lay me low. I had believed it implicitly.

Terrorism

The hand-grenading of the Buddhist temple in My
Tho was still being talked about in Saigon, when I
returned from Dak Pek. Even more than the new
fighting in the upper Delta, it seemed on all the newsmen's tongues. It made the cease-fire even more of a
joke. What cease-fire? Seven dead, and fourteen
wounded. In a Buddhist temple while at worship.
Why? And for what? The priests had not paid their VC
taxes? Even if they paid the taxes, now, they would
have a hard time getting their congregation back into
that particular temple. It was the first such incident
since I had been there. And I was interested in observing its effect. It was particularly demeaning in the
way it made people check the exits, wherever they
happened to be sitting, no matter how they tried not

to, and look at the people around them, and check if their flanks were covered, and that their back was against a wall.

There was something embarrassing and shameful about terrorism that made people lower their eyes when they talked about it. It seemed to outrage something basic in everyone, which, each time it did, put them dangerously closer to accepting the very code of the terrorist which they detested.

The Vietnamese people I talked to about it, such as my interpreter Vo and the girls at the Continental Palace terrace, seemed to take it more as a matter of course. They shrugged, or changed the subject. But always there was that smothered embarrassed smile and downward cast of the eyes. It was curiously like talking about sex.

It was hard to know what went on in the mind of a terrorist. But in every case the terrorist seemed to carry with him like moral armor a sense of vast moral superiority which was untouchable. Which made it legitimate for him to commit his acts, and made it unnecessary for him even to rationalize them. And which made it immoral for his enemies to commit the same acts upon him, because they did not enjoy his moral position.

In her book *Fire in the Lake*, Frances Fitzgerald presents a marvelous apologia for Viet Cong and North Viet political assassination and terrorism. While attacking furiously the political assassination and terrorism of the South Viets. The VC and NV did not kill indiscriminately, she says, but carefully calculated killings for maximum political effect. Their lists of people had to undergo long bureaucratic scrutiny before being used. The killing was done in a cold-blooded, unpassionate manner by special teams. They did not torture or hurt people beforehand, and preferred the bullet as the quickest, cleanest, most decent manner of giving death. In the first place, these statements by the North Viets simply were not true. It is a textbook statement of what they wanted the world to believe about their terrorist program. How did you assassinate a person decently? Second, the whole tone of their reasoning is one of such enormous moral self-righteousness that it would be laughable if it wasn't so scary. The whole thing smacks of a schoolteacher's dissertation on the moral superiority of marital sex over unmarried sex.

The truth is, all terrorists are hired guns. It is not enough to say they are doing it in a good cause. The terrorist is willing to accept the responsibility for the lives of the people he liquidates. But he is not so willing to accept the idea that the rest of humanity secretly considers him a pariah, a being outside like a hyena or a vulture. This is the incubus his moral righteousness shields him from.

Mr. Jake

Healy's call came through almost before I was back in my room and unpacked. He had talked to "Mr. Jake," as everyone called him, and not only would Jacobson like to see me but he would like for me to come to dinner at his house that night. Healy would drop me off there, but would not be able to stay as he had two conferences to attend that night.

Saigon was taking a bit of getting used to, after the North and Dak Pek. Back inside all the feverish politics and the gossip and speculation of the newsmen, which were the basic heart of Saigon, there was this accelerated sense of everything moving more and more swiftly to a grand climax as X+60 and the day of departure approached. I stood in my window looking down in the afternoon sunlight at the animated, pulsing, honking square, and then went and put in a call to Fred Weyand.

Naturally, he was in some conference. But rather than give up the line and not be able to get another I said I would wait. Finally he came on the line. He listened quietly and without comment while I thanked him for Healy and told him my problem about the Delta. I was finding my attitude toward Weyand undergoing a change after being away in the North. So great were the admiration and respect the men who served under him had for him, so great was his influence, that I was finding it hard to think of him as my old buddy Fred from Paris. Occasionally I found myself slipping and calling him Sir. A thing I was sure he wouldn't particularly like. I told him I felt I had to get down into the Delta before I could wind up my trip. If he couldn't help me, I didn't know what else to do except rent a car, and drive it. I told him Vo my interpreter advised me against it, but was reluctantly willing to go if I paid him double his regular price, for hazardous work. I told him what Mike Healy had said about getting in touch with George Jacobson at CORDS.

He was silent a moment before he answered. When he spoke, he sounded even more tired and worn than when I had had lunch with him, but still healthy and altogether with it. He would call George Jacobson and talk to him and see what he had in mind. But he strongly advised me against trying to drive it to Can Tho, the capital. There was too much going on down there right now, too many daily truce violations. I should not go until I had talked to him. Then his voice changed. "I heard you made a little sightseeing vacation trip from Pleiku with Mike," he said. I hastened to assure him that if anything was wrong, it was my fault, not Healy's. I had practically coerced him into making the trip. It was a damned, dangerous, foolish thing to do, Weyand said. Then his voice softened. At least nobody had got hurt. "But Gloria will have my ears if she ever hears about that trip," he said with a laugh. He would talk to Jacobson. And I must promise I wouldn't go into the Delta until we'd talked. As I hung up, I couldn't help but feel a little guilty that I had coerced him a little, with the car bit.

When Healy's car picked me up in front of the enormous doors of the Continental, it was already after dark. I slipped into the seat beside him without saying much. I had already made up my mind I was not going to make any more failed efforts at thanking him. I thought Healy seemed relieved that I wasn't. I told him what Weyand had said about our escapade, and he grinned. He was in less bad over that, he said, than he had been over the time he got Fritzie the German to sing *Deutschland über Alles* to the Hungarians and the Poles.

Jacobson's house was an ordinary villa-type Saigon house, well guarded by Viet MPs. Inside, it was decorated with Oriental statues, brass bowls and *objets,* lacquered inlay landscapes, and bric-a-brac Jacobson obviously had collected. Healy stayed only for one polite drink, before going to his first meeting.

Jacobson was a big man, with big purple circles of fatigue under his eyes and what might be the beginning of ill health, if he did not let up on his work load. He did not appear to be letting up. And he looked like he didn't give a damn. His hair was rumpled and grizzled. And he appeared perpetually pressed for time, as if even at home he could not let up from the schedule that kept him running all day. If his personal style was abrupt and irascible, it was this time pressure, his eyes seemed to say.

Jacobson had been thrown up into a kind of instant if brief fame in the press during Tet of 1968, when an MP in the Embassy grounds had tossed him up a .45 to shoot an armed VC sapper coming up the stairs of his Embassy villa to the second floor. It was the kind of story that made good newspaper copy for one issue. When I mentioned I had read the story and admired him for it, he waved it away with an impatient snarl. That was nothing. The kind of thing anybody did when they had to. I made the point that not everybody was capable of it. And he snarled it away again. Then they would be dead, he said. And that would be it. For them. In any case, that kind of kid stuff was not what we were here to talk about.

He was a blunt man, he said, and he would get to the point quickly. He had something arranged, and on the fire, that might be just exactly what I was looking for in the short time I seemed to have. But first he had a few things to say, and he wanted to say them.

He began to talk, and we talked through our drinks

and into the dining room, talked right through the dinner, talked through the coffee after, and talked until I was practically outside the door, where his car took me back to the hotel.

In the first place, he wanted me to know that he had not been much in favor of bringing another reporter out to Vietnam. Even if the reporter was a novelist, and claimed to be writing an unbiased view. There were too damned many reporters already. And none of them was willing to risk his neck to write an unbiased view. All they were interested in was scandal, and finding some way to make the United States look bad again. Because that was popular. Fine. That was their right. But there was always scandal in a big outfit, and there was always some way of making the United States look bad. In spite of all that, he had this thing arranged for me if I wanted to take it. But he had one or two things more to say, first.

I was looking at probably the last, sole surviving believer in the domino theory, Jacobson said with a tired grin. And no matter what had been *said,* nothing had been *done* to make the domino theory invalid. By hook or crook, scab or grab, the North Viets were now in possession of approximately half of South Vietnam. What they were starting to call the Third Vietnam. They were also in possession of most of Laos, and over half of Cambodia. There was no reason at all to assume they would stop there. And there was no reason in the world to assume they would stop with Cambodia. In the north and east of Thailand infiltration groups were already operating, and already strong enough to make travel without armed escort impossible. And beyond Thailand there was nothing but the mountains of Burma, and then India.

You in your trips around, Jacobson said. You've seen what they're doing in the Third Vietnam. Road systems, military installations, airstrips, rocket sites. They were doing the same in Laos and Cambodia. They were beginning to move in political cadres. Setting up administrative systems. Setting up a school system. Already. And all contrary to the cease-fire agreement. And now the word was they were beginning to bring in women. Single women. In work battalions. Future wives for the State, all right there and waiting.

Jacobson was beginning to look tired. Along with all this, we had talked about other, perhaps deeper, more philosophical things, too. Like what makes a man, in any army, like and prefer to be a soldier. On the other hand, he grinned, no one should write South Vietnam off. Our American commitment, with all its fumbles, the bungling, the mistakes, the total lack of understanding, the enormous cost, the American lives lost, had done something. It had given these people time. Time to grow together, time to train, time to build themselves a damn good army. Contrary to the newspapers, there were an awful lot of people in South Vietnam who really did not want to live under the North Viet Communist system. Our involvement had given those people a chance to do it on their own. If, and there were a lot of ifs, they could continue to develop, and we could continue to help them from outside, they might be able to hold out indefinitely. He for one was committed to that. He did not intend to go home, and he never expected to leave here.

We were long past our coffee by this time, and I was almost at the door when he told me what I had come to find out about. The chief American military advisor to the Delta IV Corps command was making a grand inspection tour of all the Delta provinces to say good-by to all the province chiefs. It was a three- or four-day tour, and it was already one day gone, but if I wanted I could ride along with him for the rest of it. I would get to see more of the Delta than I would ever get to see any other way, or at any other time.

If I wanted to go, I had a reservation on the Air America flight to Can Tho tomorrow at nine in the morning. I could pick up my ticket at the airport.

Delta

From reading about it, one gets the idea the Mekong Delta is a lush jungled area, reclaimed for rice growing. Nothing's further from the fact. More than anything, in the dry season, it reminded me of the flat upland areas of Montana and Wyoming, and parts of northern New Mexico. Except for the system of canals and irrigation ditches, it would be an arid brushgrown chaparral. From the air it was a vast brown plain of patches in varying shades, but always brown. The only relief, the only green visible at the end of the dry season was in the towns and along the canals, and the faint green threads of the ditches. Every few miles one or more of the great steely-sheened meandering arms of the river was in sight. Across the expanse, straight as a surveyor's plumb line, ran the famous highway Route 4 to Can Tho, our destination, fading into the distance haze in both directions.

I was the only passenger on the little six-passenger Air America Pilatus Porter, and the American pilot obligingly pointed out the sights for me. Ben Tre, the town the American colonel reported, "We had to destroy it to save it." The Truc Giang peninsula: about 90% of the Viet Minh went North to fight from here. Naturally, it had one of the highest absentee landlord counts in French Vietnam. Over My Tho, the pilot tipped us, and we hung and swung stationary as My Tho rotated beneath us on its Song My Tho mouth of the Mekong. My Tho was where the Buddhist pagoda had been hand-grenaded four days before.

My entry into this formidable area was from the CORDS office in Saigon, with an assist by General Weyand. CORDS, which was the acronym for Civil Operations and Rural Development Support, infiltrated throughout the MACV structure, so that wherever there was a military advisor there was a corresponding CORDS representative. In Can Tho one of the main preoccupations of the CORDS office was with the new land reform program, which was to be so important to the Delta, and that was one of the things I wanted to take a look at.

Theoretically, it was possible to drive all over the Delta. Except for two or three areas like the U-Minh Forest on the western coast and the Plain of Reeds to the north. The towns were all more or less government-controlled, and government forces patrolled and controlled the main roads, at least in the daytime. People drove it all the time. But the flat, burnt, unvarying scenery was boring in the heat, the distances to be covered uncomfortable in a hot eye-smoldering car. At night the Viet Cong were prone to come out into the villages and hamlets and terrorize them and collect at gun point the VC imposed taxes in rice. The local militia would either put up a fight or flee. Many of the towns which held substantial military forces would be mortared in the night, some night after night. Sporadically in the daytime the VC would bombard a government post or mine a bridge or crossroad or knock off a loaded bus or car. The cease-fire, which had stopped some of the action in the Central Highlands and along the Annam coast, had almost no effect on the VC in the Delta. It was dull and profitless to drive the lonely flat road mile after mile, unless you met up with the VC. If you met the VC, it was likely to be too exciting and too profitable. Looking down on it, I was glad I wasn't having to drive it.

Below us in the plane the great flat gray-brown table stretched away as far as the eye could see, absolutely flat, flat as any desktop. It seemed to have a brooding, mysterious visual silence about it, perceptible to the eyeball rather than to the ear. The famous canals were much farther apart than I had thought, the areas between interlaced with the green threads of irrigation ditches. All the arboreal vegetation grew along the larger canals, and cluster after cluster of houses formed a continuous double band of habitation along them, beyond which the verdure cover extended only a few yards. The rest was scrub or paddy fields, most of them dry and brown now in the height of the dry season. Through all this the broad arms of the Mekong wandered lazily, either directly beneath us or glinting in the distance. We were never far from one. When we were above one, sweep sampans and motor sampans moved along it. In the notebook on my knee I printed in large letters, "Conrad country!"

Finally, the pilot pointed out Can Tho to me in the distant heat haze, and began to descend.

Teeth

I have found, over my many years of travel, that you can generally pretty well tell the state of a nation's affluence, and of its social development, by the state of that nation's teeth.

Good dentists are a lot like fine whores and good oil drillers, in that they flock to where the gold is. If the teeth of a nation's leaders and low-level government bureaucrats are in general well-formed, and sexually attractive, this means the nation is affluent. If the teeth of its workers, merchants, soldiers and prisoners are also in fine shape, it means the nation has reached a pretty high level of social advancement. None of this is due to diet, you understand, but to the advent—or home-growth—of superior dentists.

By this criterion, the United States is the most affluent and most socially advanced nation on earth. We have our Appalachian snaggles, our ghetto stubs, and our Mississippi Delta yellow fangs, but in general our workers and lower classes have the best dental work of any in the world. The Germans however, with the rise of the mark, are coming on fast, and there is a noticeable increase in the beauty of the teeth of German tourists, as there is increase of the tourists themselves. The Japanese teeth—though admittedly they perhaps have a built-in natural disadvantage—are improving also. But the marked difference in shapeliness between the teeth of Japanese leaders, industrialists, and businessmen and those of the Japanese worker indicate a level of social advancement that is still not much past the feudal.

In certain of the so-called Socialist Republics there has been a trend of late for the leaders and bureaucrats to go around displaying sets of misaligned, decayed and snaggly teeth in order to show they are for the people and of the people. I do not think this tactic will have any long-range success, however. You can fool the people about their politics forever but not about the horror of their teeth—not if you let them see US movies.

In South Vietnam I saw the most awful collection of rotting, decayed and misshapen teeth it's ever been my sad duty to observe. And, if their returning prisoners at Quang Tri are examples, the North Viets are not any better off. This, of course, does not apply to South Viet leaders and their expensive wives, all of whom go to Hong Kong or America for their teeth, and amongst them have some of the most beautiful sets ever to appear on US TV. But it applies to the poor, the fighting Army, the beggars, the young hookers, and even to the merchants.

But in the matter of teeth, the Vietnamese have other ramifications. It is not only the chewing of the betel, which turns the teeth a bright blood-red, fading to rust-red depending upon how lately the bearer of the teeth has chewed. The Viets have also developed a custom of lacquering the teeth of their women a jet-black. Fortunately, this custom seems to be fading out among the young, but at first it is very disconcerting to go up to some Viet lady in a shop and have her give you a big smile that at first appears to be a black hole in her face, and only on closer inspection turns out to be black-lacquered teeth. And you never do get over it entirely.

There are many theories as to the origin of this custom. They run all the way from one which says it was originally done to protect a set of particularly beautiful teeth, to one which says it was done by ladies at the time of their marriage to make them sexually unattractive to other men. There is one that it was done by high-born ladies as a mark of caste, and one that it was only done by the low-born and was a mark of ignorance.

In any case, the custom proves conclusively just how sexually attractive and unattractive teeth and the lack of teeth are. Still, I do not think it will ever be taken up and become popular in our country. Unless the young women in our colleges adopt it as a form of protest against being sexual objects. In that case there will be a big economic boom for Vietnamese lacquerists in the US.

The Seven Mountains

The name had a Conradian flavor to it, and called up a romantic feeling about the inscrutable mystic Orient, its age-old concern with the magic cabalistic number 7. In the heyday of the American involvement, the US 9th Division fought the North Viets around there, and all along the border east toward Chau Doc, and fought major battles at Hong Ngu. In Saigon and all over the North at Pleiku, at Hue, in Da Nang and Nha Trang, I kept running into US personnel who had fought there, and who talked of the toughness of the fighting and the harshness of the terrain, adding to the mystique the place engendered. All those I talked to about it carried their own personal mythic mystique about it in their eyes, adding still further to my own.

When you think of the name, you envision a small, tight, nearly circular, forested range, altogether and all of a piece, with seven separate heads rising out of the main wooded mass, above the plain below, the whole dark and brooding and ominous.

It is not like that at all, when you see it. The mountains are scattered over a roughly twenty-mile area, with the plain flowing like a sea in-between and around the separate heads. At least two are little better than knolls, and there appear to be nine, not seven. But two are not counted—perhaps to facilitate the use of the magic number 7. All are tortured, burnt cone shapes, irregular and black and forbidding on the plain that flows around them, ominous enough and looking like cinders, where woods do not cover them. Two are double-headed, and count as four among the magic 7, and there most of the fighting took place in the past. The town of Tri Ton lies just about in the middle of them, and was where the recent mortaring had been happening. The town of Tinh Bien, often under attack by the Communists, lay just at the northeast entrance of them.

Travels with a General

There are helicopters and helicopters, and the generals get the best ones. This had been told me by a disgruntled young chopper pilot up in I Corps, who had once flown for a general but been reduced to flying what he called a deathtrap piece of tin, for infractions he did not specify. The principle held true in IV Corps in the Delta, just as it had done in II Corps, and I Corps.

This was my third general in as many weeks, and I was beginning to get used to them. They might all have their personal idiosyncrasies that had to be indulged. And might be too used to having their creature comforts taken care of for them. But those I met deserved their rank and were good solid professionals. Men who often had to carry sole responsibility for decisions that could prolong or terminate the lives of many of their fellow citizens. And who were well aware of it. As far as I was concerned they deserved the best helicopters. Especially, since I would be riding them, too.

I was arriving in the late morning, and so was missing the first day and a half of the four-day tour. But I was catching the part I wanted most, which was the trip to the north of the Delta near the fighting. Once we were airborne, the general began filling me in on what was the situation in his command.

His name was Frank Blazey. He was the only West

Pointer among the four MACV Regional commanders. He was a blocky, muscled man, brave as hell and
tough as nails I was told. "Windy, but tough, old
devil," was the exact phrase. At first meeting, there
was something a bit prissy, pedantic, something of
the paternalistic schoolteacher about him. But after
a while you began to get down under that.

The Delta, Blazey felt, had been changed the least
by the cease-fire, of the four Regional commands. The
big battles along the Cambodian border had stopped.
But the Delta had been the stamping ground of the
guerrillas since the days when they were called the
Viet Minh, and the cease-fire had not changed that
part much. They were still roaming the countryside
in bands of platoon and company strength. Deftly, on
a map on his knees, he showed me the basic strate-
gies. On the southwest coast was a huge area called
the U-Minh Forest, which wasn't really a forest at all
but a great mangrove swamp. The North Viets supplied this area by sea with men, arms, and munitions,
and from there the VC—mainly North Vietnamese
since 1968—carried the stuff overland along what was
called the Long My Corridor, into the central Delta in
Chuong Thien Province. Only last night Long My the
town had been mortared again. Six rounds, eight
wounded. Civilians. On 35 of the 53 nights since the
cease-fire began, Long My had taken VC mortar fire.
Long My was in Chuong Thien Province, forty miles
from Can Tho, and Chuong Thien was the worst province in the Delta. We would be going there later.
Blazey grinned.

He shifted the map on his knees. In the north the
present hot spots were at Tinh Bien and Tri Ton in
Chau Doc Province. At Tri Ton the North Viet Army

held the slopes of the Seven Mountains, and the government troops held the tops of them and the villages at their feet. At Tinh Bien the North Viets were pushing troops against and around Nui Giai Mountain. Lately, they had begun pushing more troops in around Hong Ngu. Strategically, the idea was to open up—or reopen—an entry port down into the central Delta, that would augment the Long My Corridor in the southwest. They had had one on the Bassac River arm of the Mekong, called "The Sampan Road" by the troops, but the South Viets had closed it back in December and January.

Two weeks ago the VC in the Seven Mountains had hit a schoolyard in Tri Ton with a 75 recoilless rifle and killed a couple of teachers and half a dozen kids. This had seemed a clear-cut truce violation and the Canadians and Indonesians agreed to investigate it. The Poles and Hungarians had refused, on grounds of personal safety; which was their right; they had been doing this more and more lately, especially when the violations were clearly NVA or VC. The Canadians had shamed them into going as "Observers," if not as a full-scale "Investigation," which meant there would be no official report, but they hoped to establish a precedent for later. Since the arrival of the ICCS in Tri Ton, there had been violations four days in a row, with both 82-mm mortars and 122-mm rockets. Two people wounded on March 18th. Two wounded on the 19th. One killed, four wounded on the 20th. Two killed, fourteen wounded on the 21st, yesterday. Yesterday's rounds had gone right into the JMC compound, where, naturally, the NVA and VC contingents had never arrived. It was located across town, away from the ICCS. Even so, now of course the Poles and Hungarians were threatening to pull out and leave. Blazey grinned at me again, and folded his map. "We are getting a little tetchy about people back home who call us the evil villians out here," he said.

I just nodded. Was there any chance of our getting into Tri Ton, I asked him. He shook his head. No. And he couldn't take me in there. We were going to go to Chau Doc the town and have lunch with the Chau Doc province chief and province commander, to say good-by. Then we would stop off ten minutes at Chi Lang, the division HQ for the troops fighting below Tinh Bien. And wind up with a visit to Long Xuyen, capital of An Giang Province, the Hoa Hao country. That was our schedule. Unless, of course, something untoward happened.

The first untoward thing happened at Chau Doc. We were seated to a Vietnamese gourmet lunch in the cool HQ villa on the bank of the Mekong, when a telephone rang somewhere. A minute later a young American aide from the Consulate came rushing in excitedly, and said the North Viets had just dropped eight 122 rockets into a crowded Cambodian refugee camp at Tan Chau ten miles north on the other river. Twenty houses down. Two killed. About thirty wounded. The young vice-consul was a pretty old Vietnam hand, but he looked shocked even so. I saw Blazey's jaw tighten as he sat back down to his lunch.

Later, when I could, I asked him why. Why bombard a refugee camp that had no military targets or significance? I couldn't see any point. The reason, Blazey said, was to terrorize the people into leaving the camp. When the fighting came to their area, they left their land and came to our camps. The North Viets wanted them to go back to their land and start raising the crops the North Viets needed to supply them.

The second untoward thing occurred in the air, about two minutes after we had left Chi Lang. In Chi Lang, I had sat for thirty minutes (not ten) in an HQ bunker and listened to Blazey lecture the South Viet colonel commanding the 44th Military Area HQ, about not putting on a full-scale attack with his troops up toward Tinh Bien. The colonel, named Ninh, was furious over the harassment and casualties he was taking from the North Viet pressure, and wanted to confront them in a pitched battle. Moreover, he was absolutely sure he could whip the NVA troops in front of him. Since his command had a high degree of autonomy, he could actually make the attack, if he chose to. Patiently, over and over, Blazey explained that that was exactly what the North Viets wanted, so that they would have a truce violation of their own to publicize. A major one. Blazey's patience with the furious Viet colonel was astonishing. Finally he exacted a promise not to fight from Ninh, and shook hands and left smiling. But once he was back in the air he began to swear. Before he could finish swearing and tell me whether it was Colonel Ninh or the North Viets he was mad at, the radio came in on our ears and it was Tri Ton calling for Blazey.

Tri Ton had just been hit again with 82-mm mortars. An ARVN captain with the JMC had had both legs blown off. There were several other wounded. But no US personnel. They were trying to plot the trajectory of the mortar path. They knew he was in the area. Did he want to come in.

I listened to Blazey talking to them in a military jargon I only half understood. It certainly did not seem to me like any cease-fire around here, I remember thinking. Then Blazey said he was coming in. But he wanted them off the air, so as not to give any radio information to an enemy transmitter. He would not come in at the regular helicopter pad, but would land in the field behind the JMC compound. Since the VC would probably have no prearranged mortar setting for that. They should have a jeep waiting for him.

Then he switched off the external radio band and began giving his pilot instructions.

We would go in low level. And fast. 110 or 120. The pilot should hug the mountainside on our right until he was right on the town. As soon as Blazey and I were on the ground, the pilot would lift right off so as not to draw fire. He could land at the ICCS pad across the city to save fuel. The enemy wouldn't be mortaring the Poles and Hungarians. Also it might make the enemy think the chopper wasn't coming back. But he should be back for us in exactly twenty minutes, on the ground. In front of us the child pilot was nodding his head and saying Roger into his mouth mike.

Blazey looked up and for a moment looked as though he was supremely happy to be doing something else besides cautioning Viet colonels not to fight. He grinned at me. I was going to get to go into Tri Ton after all, he said.

Fire at Tri Ton

It was an eight-minute run from where we were to the pasture we landed in. It did not seem to me that we could be more than thirty-five or forty feet off the ground. The pilot followed his instructions exactly. The sense of speed and excitement was astonishing, and irresistible. The ominous black cones of part of the Seven Mountains had been on our right front since before landing at Chi Lang. Now we swung in toward them and went into a long finger-valley of plain that ran between two of them, the largest of them all, Nui Cam, 2329 ft., on our right, and the second largest, An Lac, 1926 ft., directly in front of us. At the face of An Lac, running straight into it seemingly, we made a sharp right-angle turn to the left, canting the helicopter ninety degrees, and followed the mountain's bottom edge around. And directly in front, the town of Tri Ton appeared in a pocket of flat plain with still another of the Seven Mountains beyond it. Blazey took off his earphones and unfastened his seat belt, and motioned for me to do the same.

At the pasture, beside a weary-looking old farmhouse that had been hit by mortars several times, we were hardly down the step and on the ground before the helicopter was whirring off at an acute angle. In the trees by the farmhouse a jeep was waiting for us. We jogged over to it, with Blazey's South Viet aide.

209

The jeep was driven by a young US colonel named Short, who wore the orange armband of the four-power JMC. He rolled us two hundred yards along a rutty dirt road and slowed up for us to look at the building that had taken the mortar rounds. The rounds had landed in the courtyard, and had smashed windows and doors, and fragments had pockmarked the walls. All of the blood had not yet been washed up. The legless ARVN captain and the others had been taken away, and were being flown out by helicopter to the hospital in Chau Doc. Colonel Short did not know whether the ARVN captain was going to make it. Excitedly, he reached over the back of his seat to shake hands with me, warmly.

A hundred yards farther along, at a sandbagged HQ bunker that was nevertheless not immune to a direct hit from on top, Blazey and Short pored over a map. I did not understand the mathematics of plotting the path of a mortar round back to the tube, and did not feel like asking in the midst of the excitement, but Colonel Short had already done it, and now was checking out his findings with Blazey, who was pleased. The fire was coming from a spot on the side of Nui Co To, the mountain we had seen beyond the town coming in. Short added that the government observation post on top of Nui Co To had been under direct ground attack for five days. Some of the younger officers offered Blazey and me cold beer from an electric icebox while Blazey and Short talked.

They were lucky they did not lose the entire GVN JMC contingent today, Short said excitedly. It was only a matter of time until this place was hit, too. He touched his orange armband. "These splendid protective insignia and a buck and a half will get you into any movie in town."

"But no popcorn," a young major said.

They had been shooting from up there for over ten years, Short said to me. They could drop one on just about any square yard of ground they wanted to, down here. But his group, being JMC, did not have any authority to take any counteraction, he added.

Blazey nodded. What had happened to the ICCS, he wanted to know. The Poles and the Hungarians had already pulled out, Short said contemptuously. They were getting into their choppers when he was trying to radio us. The Canadians and Indonesians had stayed, but now there could be no unanimous report at all, not even an Observers' report. He was angry now, as well as excited. They could be dropping a couple right on our heads right now, he said.

In that case, Blazey said, if there wasn't going to be any ICCS report, he would take the authority. He was authorizing them to get out some of the ARVN artillery units and plaster the whole side of Nui Co To. If they couldn't get the mortars, they could at least make them move away from there and shut them up. "Now we will be accused by the North Vietnamese of making another truce violation," Blazey grinned at me.

"Sir, your copter is leaving the ICCS pad," one of the younger officers said from the radio.

We shook hands all around again, warmly, in that strange density of excitement, with that strange closeness you get, and Colonel Short drove us back. Outside, the men in the compound moved quickly, with their shoulders hunched down in a peculiar way, that for me was like an old faded memory suddenly brought back fresh.

Once we were airborne, Blazey explained that the most probable reason for the attacks on Tri Ton was that it was an effort to force Colonel Ninh at Chi Lang to pull troops away from his forces in front of Tinh Bien and send them to clean out the slopes in the Seven Mountains. "Well, I guess you can honestly say you've been blooded in Vietnam, now," he grinned.

I just nodded. By the time we got to Long Xuyen for our meeting with the Hoa Hao province chief, it all seemed so very far away. I hadn't been blooded in Vietnam and we both knew it. So did the men who stayed at Tri Ton. But it was nice of him to say it.

That night at HQ in Can Tho, we learned that in fact the ARVN captain had not made it. He had died shortly after his arrival at the hospital in Chau Doc.

Chuong Thien

Blazey had told me Chuong Thien was the worst province in the Delta for security and guerrilla movement, and because of that I wanted to visit it.

Vi Thanh, the province capital, was a pleasant town, well treed and green, filled with numerous small canals, but hot and dusty now at the peak of the dry season. The province chief's headquarters was a heavily defended place, more like the ones I had seen in the North in Pleiku and Hue, than the compound of a "pacified" Delta province.

A glance at an operations map made it easy to see why. Not far to the west was the famous U-Minh Forest, the home of several major Communist bases dating back to the Viet Minh. I had flown over parts of this area already, and more than anything it resembled the Florida Everglades. From it the VC and NVA could supply, reinforce, and infiltrate all the way across the Delta to Vinh Long and Vinh Binh and Kien Hoa Provinces, almost to Saigon. Chuong Thien lay directly astraddle of this infiltration route. And so Chuong Thien became the first big bone of contention, whenever the Communists wanted to make a move eastward. And it was imperative to them to keep their supply route through it open.

Over the years attempts had been made to change this situation. But nothing had ever succeeded. Crack ARVN units had been brought in one or two at a time and given specific areas of operation around the U-Minh for short periods. Blocking attempts and a complete isolation of it had been tried. Smaller or larger task forces had been sent into the U-Minh itself to root the Communist units out. And at one point, a grandiose campaign was mounted to clear the U-Minh completely and for all time. It lasted from December 1, 1970, to November 26, 1971. Almost immediately after, the elusive VC/NVA units, undestroyed, began to regroup and reoutfit, and rebuild their infiltration route. By the 1972 spring offensive they were able to make Chuong Thien a hot spot of the lower Delta, and had remained strong ever since.

American military advisor talent had helped plan and organize this big campaign, and may have instituted it. Their men had ridden in or walked in with every combat unit. After it was over, MACV personnel had written glowing papers and bound pamphlets about the campaign's huge success. They could only be read as propaganda, in spite of the minor achievements and successes on the ground itself (which were valid enough), because the campaign obviously was a failure.

A lot of reasons for the failure to reduce the U-Minh have been put forward. The ARVN units the GVN brought in stayed only for short periods, and were never in sufficient strength. Their fixed, specific areas of operation allowed the more fluid VC/NVA units to move on to areas where they found less counterpressure. Perhaps the GVN felt it could never commit more troops from somewhere else at any given time. But when they did put on the big U-Minh Campaign, it was handled badly. The enemy easily moved away from any decisive contact until he had numbers and terrain on his side before he would turn and fight. Nobody seems to have thought of the idea of targeting a crack ARVN unit with firepower and numerical superiority onto a specific enemy unit on a one-on-one basis, with orders to pursue it until its combat effectiveness was smashed.

And now in March of 1973, after more than seven weeks of cease-fire, Chuong Thien was in a continuous state of semisiege. Long My had been shelled with mortars the night before. And nearly every other night. Roads to the town of Kien Thien in the south were interdicted, and it had to be supplied by hook. The VC held thirty percent of the terrain. From this they sallied forth at night to frighten and tax the government hamlets. The political assassination campaign in the province had continued right on through the cease-fire, and showed signs that it would be picking up when the Americans left. In the past year Chuong Thien had lost its ten best Regional Forces company commanders by assassination. Four top village chiefs were dead, by assassination. Whenever a man showed leadership and talent and began to rise, the assassination teams went after him. This put a premium on men, even amongst the bravest and toughest, who would accept the jobs.

In a way, if you did not care too much about being too careful, Chuong Thien could almost be taken as a microcosm of the whole American adventure in Vietnam.

Now hard-core VC were coming home and moving back into their villages, unarmed. They were family members. And they had the brass, the raw guts, to say the war was over, they were going to help rebuild. They would say this after a village ten kilometers away had been mortared the night before. There was no doubt about why they were really coming back.

In the meantime, since the 1972 Easter offensive, the GVN had adopted a policy of trying to hold the land by a system of fixed "Operational Bases," manned by small units of the Regional Forces or People's Forces, thus giving away both mobility and initiative to the enemy. This might work up in I Corps or II Corps, but in the Delta all it did was tie RF and PF units to their little forts, and an area extending about one kilometer around, leaving them there where the VC/NVA units could bypass them, or knock them off piecemeal one by one whenever they wanted to make a demonstration.

Even Vi Thanh the province headquarters was no longer immune to mortaring. They had had one just ten days ago. "Doesn't it get to you? Like that?" I asked the American four-power JMC representative, a young lt colonel named Bob Meese. "Yeah, you know," he said. "They could drop a series in on us today. Right now. But you know and I know that 99.9% of them aren't going to hit yourself. Have to be a very lucky one." There were mortar fragment holes in two walls of the living room of his tiny villa inside the high-fenced compound. All the rest of the damage had been repaired from the mortaring of ten days ago, but he had left those there, to remind him. They made for better ventilation, and he could use them for peepholes to see across the compound, and watch who brought what local girl in, he said. "And yet, you know, I hate to leave. There's a lot of good here, too. The people really don't want the VC. They aren't poor, you know. There's prosperity. The new land reform program is working, the 'Land to the Tiller' program. There's a lot less corruption. I'm really going to hate to go and leave them."

He walked me out across the road from the fence to the blacktop pad where the helicopter was waiting. As I was fastening my tricky seat belt, something fell through the air and clanged against the copter ski and clattered onto the blacktop. I looked down and saw a rock the size of my fist lying on the blacktop between the skids. Two Viet men were walking along the dirt road across the tiny canal. "Hey! You son of a bitch!" Meese yelled furiously. He had already charged around the copter, and stood shouting something in Viet at the men. They stood looking at him a moment and then walked on. He came back around the nose, grinning lamely. "I can't go chasing them all down." I agreed. "That could just as easily have been a grenade," I said. Meese nodded, "That was what he was letting us know." "What did you say to him in Vietnamese?" I asked. He grinned belligerently. "I was just letting him know I knew who he was." He backed away to the road so we could take off, and stood waving.

Fear

That night I lay in bed and thought about Meese going to bed night after night in Vi Thanh not knowing if he would wake up to a mortaring. And that got me to thinking about fear.

There had been a little drinking in the bar after dinner and one of the administrative officers talking to some of us had said to me with a smile, "I wouldn't have gone up there to Tri Ton like that." I looked around at the others and said sure he would, if it had been an order. Oh, yes; if it had been an order, he said. But I had not been ordered to go. I wanted to go. I had said so. I grinned and admitted that I had wanted to go. And then suddenly I shut up—because I did not want to admit out loud that I did not know why I wanted to go.

Anyway, I added, it was not the same thing as an infantryman who had to stay there day after day, week after week, watching his percentages chances diminish. Everybody agreed to that, and the subject changed.

I did not think it made Meese afraid to go to bed in Vi Thanh. And I did not think it would make me afraid. But it is hard to know what makes one man afraid, and not another. I had not been afraid when I went into Tri Ton with General Blazey. And I had not been afraid on the trip to Dak Pek with Mike Healy. I had honestly not been afraid when I vaguely saw and then heard the falling object clang against the helicopter and looked down to see if it was a grenade.

Usually fear came to me when I was alone, and there was nothing to do, like those last few moments before going to sleep at night; when I was going to do something the next day and imagined all the things that could happen to me, or when I had already done something and imagined all the things that *might have* happened to me. Then I could become terrified. I had been terribly afraid the night before I flew up to Dak Pek with Healy. And I had been terribly afraid the night after I had flown into Tri Ton with Blazey. So afraid I was ashamed of myself.

And yet that fear was oddly seductive. It was a strange thing, fear. It wasn't always so unpleasant. It could be as exciting as sex. And in the same way. If all the factors were right, fear could be terribly exciting. So exciting you could get hooked on it like a drug. And want to do it again. Like sex.

I had been made terribly afraid the first day I was back in Saigon, when I first heard of the hand-grenading of the Buddhist temple. I had gone back to my room in the Continental Palace and stood for a long time looking down at the bustling, crowded square, wondering at how bestial men could be to each other and still enjoy it. I felt as if I had been personally raped by the VC hand-grenade tossers.

And when I looked back up, I thought for a split-second flash I had glimpsed again my hairy, jug-eared, bucktoothed little friend in the branches, among the leaves of the big tree outside, his tiny eyes glinting, his small body bouncing up and down excitedly.

I had seen my hairy little pal again the night before I went to Dak Pek. And I had glimpsed him again the night after I got back from Tri Ton. I still did not know why I wanted to go to Dak Pek and Tri Ton. And I did not know what my hairy little friend meant or stood for.

I could remember being terribly afraid under mortar barrages in World War II. Getting to shoot back at the enemy and hurt him had helped that fear a lot. Anyway, I was younger. Back then, I had been afraid of dying without having made my voice heard in the world, without having made the fact of my existence at least known. I did not want to be lumped namelessly together with a lot of dead heroes who got remembered only collectively. A perhaps legitimate vanity.

But I had not been terrified when I was wounded, or even much afraid. Afterward, I had been afraid I might get hit again, before I could get out of there, legitimately and honorably. I thought that would be the most unholy, Godless irony. And I had seen it happen to men.

But in those days I had never touched on this odd conspiratorial physiological alliance between fear and the sense of sex. And I had never seen my apelike little friend.

The Simian Figure

It was only a literary device, of course.

I hadn't really seen him. I hadn't even glimpsed him from my eye corner. I wasn't even sure I had imagined him, and made him up, on the scene in Vietnam at the actual time, as I wrote I had. Perhaps I had invented him later, at the time of the writing.

But all of that didn't really matter. He was just as real.

Whether I actually saw him as a hallucination in my real eye, or imagined him at the time of the experience, or whether I invented him later when writing about the experience, he was just as authentic. From somewhere down there, in some subsurface part of me, he had drifted up in that dreamlike way, worming his way past the grid-filter I used to keep out the trash or the too-terrifying. An unreadable metaphor. Indecipherable, because being unreadable was part of his very function. I didn't know what he stood for, and I couldn't know. If I ever did know, certainly the answer would be trite, and his emotional usefulness would cease.

Surely, he wasn't death. Or, at least, not only just death. Death certainly carried with it some of the ridiculous ugliness, as well as the animal wisdom, that he had. And surely he wasn't fear. Though he carried about his person some of the hairy, squawky, smelly, shrewd selfishness of fear. Certainly he was

sly. And certainly he was a clown. And certainly he
was scary. I had the awful feeling that he was laughing at me, at us.

He could pass as a caricature, a cartoon of all
humanity. And with his pea-brained sense of humor,
that seemed to be just what he was doing. Could he be
a symbol of the race, and our needs for fury and danger and fear and their excitements? Maybe he was a
mirror image of myself? Myself before I shaved all
over and put on airs and clothes, and pretended to be
different? Maybe it was him I was trying to encounter
face to face when I went to Dak Pek and Tri Ton.

Whatever he was, I had him. And now that I had
him, probably I would have to go on exploring him,
and trying to figure out what he stood for, forever.
Like one of those lovable dear awful old friends who
are always turning up when you least want to see
them. The ones you can bet will always appear when
you are trying most to impress somebody else. The
ones you are always happy to see and hate to have run
into.

Land Reform

After a second day of visiting province capitals with
Blazey, I begged off on the third day. I had now traveled almost all of the Delta except the eastern section
around My Tho. I had been from Rach Gia on the
western coast in Kien Giang Province to Sa Dec to
Moc Hoa in Kien Tuong Province up in the Ele-

phant's Foot country on the Cambodian border. And except for the Tri Ton side trip, an accident, the visits to the relatively pacified provinces were no longer giving me anything new or useful. So I spent my third day in the Delta looking into the land reform program around Can Tho.

The CORDS people were very proud of "their" new land reform program, and had put a great deal of heart and sweat into it. I armed myself with half a dozen pamphlets on land reform, and sat down in a quiet corner of the office to read them. CORDS itself was in the process of a major changeover, which would take place on the day the US military left. On that day CORDS, without the MACV structure as a backup framework, would become RRO (pronounced Arrow, in acronym style), a whole new, and newly structured, outfit. Mostly everyone would keep the same place and job, but it meant a considerable shakedown and a lot of work. In spite of that, after I had digested—or anyway half digested—the land reform pamphlets, they gave me a young man and a jeep to go out into the field and talk to the peasants myself.

The young man was so conscientious it was painful. He was also defensive from the very start. Reporters were clearly some kind of curse to him. I was beginning to think more and more how little I would like being a reporter for my lifework. Everybody hated to see you coming. The young CORDS man had brought along a Vietnamese interpreter, to make doubly sure I could not say he was editing what the peasants told me. We drove out five and ten and fifteen miles into the countryside, along three different roads, stopping at random villages and hamlets along the way. I chose my own spots to stop.

In fact, it was about the pleasantest trip I made in Vietnam. There was not even a faint hint of danger, as there had been on Route 1 at the Pass of Clouds, or in Vi Thanh yesterday. The roads almost always ambled alongside small, lazy canals, or along larger canals and equally lazy rivers. We were almost always under the single-canopy vegetation cover. We had our lunch of "Chinese soup," rice and stir-fried vegetables at a tiny soup-shop restaurant in some quiet village. It was peculiar but only from the air could you have believed that by far the greatest percentage of the land was treeless. It was easy to see why newsphotos of Vietnam always gave the impression of one vast jungle.

The peasants we talked to, stopping here and there at random, were pleased and happy with the new land reform. They were kindly, friendly people, notable mainly for their fine, well-developed musculature and their terribly, woefully bad teeth. Many would go into their houses and bring out their new deeds to show us. Under the newest land reform (replacing another, less workable, much more corrupt land reform instituted some years back) the peasant who submitted a claim, and could prove he was working the land he claimed, was given legal title to the land in the form of a deed which was registered at the nearest local land office. The maximum he could hold was 15 hectares. (The old maximum had been 100 hectares, and had been one of the causes for the high amount of corruption, apparently.) The peasants set a great store by these deeds and land titles, and in the

Delta provinces which were militarily secure, the giving and registering of them was making inroads on the Viet Cong infrastructure's power.

It got easy to tell the smaller, poorer refugee houses from the houses that had stood a long time. There were usually two or three permanent houses for every new refugee house. The refugee homes were always much smaller, and jerry-built out of flimsier materials. Always the refugees came from five or six miles away, and trekked back each day to work their land and return each night to the better protected areas. It was possible to live on their new land, but the VC were inclined to come through every so often. Also, there was the problem of mines, always dangerous and nerve-racking when there were children around, playing.

However much good it did toward beating back the Viet Cong, which was not much unless there were troops around to provide the necessary security, the new land reform program was a great success in itself and was making the government popular in Can Tho's Phong Dinh Province, at least.

But Can Tho's Phong Dinh, being the Delta's capital province, was extraordinarily secure. One could not help thinking about all the sorrier, unhappier, other ones, where the land reform, no matter how successful it became, simply would not be enough.

There had been no cease-fire, really. And there was no question but that the war would go right on.

Stick Mirror

On one of those last days there in the Delta I had occasion to go to Major General Nguyen Vinh Nghi's IV Corps headquarters, for something or other. Brigadier General Blazey's office was in the same building. As we drove up to the high-fence gate with its bunkers and rolls of concertina, the colonel driving us stopped and one of the Viet MPs came over to us with something in his hand. It was a three-foot hardwood stick with a framed mirror attached at right angles to its bottom end. While we waited, he passed it under the frame of the jeep, first on one side then on the other. What the hell was that all about, I asked, as the MP waved us on. Although I thought I already knew. A mirror, the colonel said. He was looking to see if we had any bombs. Every vehicle that came through that gate got examined the same way. "Even ours?" I asked. The colonel gave me a smile. "Everybody's. Hell, we examine all our own vehicles every morning to make sure nothing's been attached to them during the night before we start them." I gave him a look, and he gave me back another smile. "That's the Delta for you," he said.

Colonel's Request

That night there was a farewell party in General Blazey's mess. With X + 60 only a few days off now, advisor officers were coming in slowly from the outlying district and province headquarters getting ready to ship out, and the mess was filling up. Two officers were leaving for Saigon tomorrow and the party was for them. In addition, as an extra added attraction not on the regular billing, it was also a farewell dinner for me.

It was after the dinner, in the bar that was getting more and more crowded every night now, that I received the second of the two requests I had in Vietnam for a direct appeal to readers. A stocky, rotund, powerful-looking colonel, who was the local comic on Blazey's staff, came over to me grinning, a glass in his hand. We knew each other pretty well by now, since all my evenings in Can Tho had been spent in this same bar, laughing or being moved by his stories about the Army and the war. He had fought in the Seven Mountains with the 9th, and in III Corps with the 25th. And like most comics he was an excellent storyteller. Also like most comics, everywhere, he had the enormous suppressed belligerence of a top combat officer.

As always with a star local comic, a group followed him. He fixed me with a mellow smile over his glass and said, "Sir, are you really gonna write all this stuff up for the people back home?" I grinned and said I hoped so. Part of it, at least. "Write something from our side, Sir," he said. "Tell them back there that we're not all Frankensteins out here." I laughed and said I would, but I wasn't sure I could get anybody to print it.

"That's exactly right," the colonel said, nodding vigorously. His name was Whitted. ("Now get that name right, Sir. W-H-I-T-T-E-D.") "They probably won't. My old daddy told me not to stay in, back in 1950. In 1950 soldiers were still heroes. But in twenty years, my daddy said, they'll be shit again. Every twenty years. He said, in 1912 every store in Brownsville, Texas, carried a sign: Soldiers and dogs not allowed. But me, I wouldn't listen to him. But you tell them, Sir. Tell them Colonel Jack Whitted said for them to remember we're not all Draculas."

While the others all laughed, and I laughed too, I said I would do my best to get his statement printed. ("Then get that name right, now, Sir. Whitted. W-H-I-T-T-E-D. Not Whitehead.")

The next day at breakfast news had come in that a People's Forces platoon had been wiped out down south in Ba Xuyen Province. Twenty men. An OB operational base overrun.

Leavetaking

Two young lieutenant colonels were on the Air America commercial flight back to Saigon. The famous X

+6o day of departure was only three days off now. The two of them were shipping out a day ahead.

Over the roar of the motor I talked to them. Both were sorry to be leaving. And both were irritated because they were being sent to Saigon two days before leaving. What would they do in Saigon for two days? Both said they would rather have stayed in their district capitals down in IV Corps. VC mortars or no VC mortars. Both of them looked drawn, and tightly thin in the face.

It was not that they did not want to get back home, one said; but that they had made so many close associations down here. The other nodded. Someday, the first said, he was going to come back here. Say in four or five years. And check the place out. See what had happened. See all his friends. He was coming back even if he had to do it on his own leave time.

As I have said, it was a comment I had heard many times, over and over, during my stay.

In Saigon everywhere there was a feeling of closing up shop. A final closing. There had not been many US soldiers walking the streets when I had left for Can Tho, and now there were even fewer. The flood of civilian workers, and their families, still coming in on the wave of economic development the American government had promised, had visibly grown. The fat white thighs of the wives and daughters in their shorts still looked incongruous, and stuck out like a sore thumb all over the shopping center of downtown Saigon. They were buying everything.

I found I was glad to be leaving. Things had changed drastically in just the short time I had been there. I was too green a hand to know if they had changed for the better or the worse. But I was depressed. The heat and so much traveling were beginning to get to me, and I was suffering from diarrhea about half the time.

By accident my departure date had coincided with that of the Army, March 28th, but the Army date had been put back one day, two weeks before when the North Viets refused to turn over a prisoner list. I saw no reason to change mine.

I spent my last two days loafing, and looking at the nude pictures in old copies of *Penthouse Magazine* that had found their way to the street vendors. I had one last dinner with Fred and Arline Weyand, at Weyand's quarters. Arline had come over from Bangkok to fly back home with the general. I tried to thank them for the truly invaluable help they had been to me. Without them I would never have got to make the trip. It was Fred who had initially suggested that I go back the other way, via Hawaii. Since I had to go to New York anyway. He thought I ought to spend a few days in Hawaii, and look it over, and write a piece about that. That was something he would really like to read, he said. I told them that I had decided to take his advice.

But other than that decision I really didn't feel like doing any work. I did have one last conversation with Mr. Jacobson. He said, in essence, that he felt he could give it as his considered opinion that the American involvement had been worth it. In spite of the enormous cost to us, our incredible blunders, the gross mistakes we had made, our unbelievable naiveté. We had given the South Viets the time they needed. And we had prevented the loss of Southeast Asia. Now it

was up to them. He volunteered that he probably
needed to believe this, but said he seriously believed
it just the same.

Plane Out

The big civilized-looking Pan-Am 747 looked as out of
place among the dusty revetments and camouflaged
aircraft as if it had landed in an Eskimo igloo village
near the North Pole. I had a final hassle with the
customs. I had not saved the teller's slips each time I
cashed in dollars for piastres at the bank. I was saved
by the tiny Viet Pan-Am hostess who was escorting
me. Her black eyes snapping, she tied into the stubborn young sergeant in Vietnamese so loudly a crowd
collected. He wilted visibly, and when I showed my
press card, let me through. All sweetness again, she
gave me a radiant smile and refused a big tip I tried
to give her. At the foot of the stairs I shook her hand,
wondering what would happen to her if the Communists took over, and climbed the two-story staircase—
right on up, and out of Vietnam.

The huge tourist cabin was only about half loaded.
Just about all of the passengers were service personnel. Even the ones in civilian clothes were service-
men, and you could tell it down the length of the
football-field-sized cabin. Huddled together like birds
were six or seven Viet girls who had married service-
men and were going to their new country for the first
time. Wedding bands were conspicuous on their

fingers. Two or three had small, half-American children with them. I plumped myself down in a civilized seat, accepted a civilized drink from a civilized American hostess, and waited to watch the coastline fade away below the thin cloud layer. I carried with me an image for the whole of Vietnam that I had seen the day before, and could not get out of my head, and probably never would get out.

The Beggar Woman

I had seen her on the Sunday, when I was walking back to the hotel from lunch. It being Sunday, there was almost nobody on the street. That made her more noticeable. I was as inured to beggars as the next man. In fact, I had just turned down two ladies with credentials, begging for some Catholic orphanage. If you did not get hardened to the beggars, you would have no money left at all—and you still would not have made a dent in them. But this one was not begging. She was standing, leaning against a shuttered Sunday storefront. I was across the street from her.

Something about her posture caught me. I thought I had never seen anyone look so beat. She stood with her head against the grillwork of the closed store, her face in the corner angle the grill made with the masonry. And she didn't move.

She seemed vaguely familiar, as if I might have seen her up the street near the hotel or the *Times* office, where the beggars congregated. She was dressed like any Viet woman, a conical straw hat, black trousers, a ragged *ao-dai*. There was no way of telling how old she was. An old US Army musette bag stuffed with something hung from her left shoulder, and she had a bundle of what looked like rags in her other arm.

I watched her a full four minutes, I timed it, and she did not move. Then her shoulders heaved themselves up slowly and fell, as if she were drawing a breath, and she became motionless again.

I wondered if she could be dying, standing there. Instinctively, like some animal reacting, I took a thousand-piastre note out of my wallet and crossed the street and touched her on the shoulder.

Her hand came up. I put the bill in it and patted her on the shoulder. Only then did her head come up, and she looked at me with such a dumb, wordless despair that it was as if someone had thrown acid in my face. I have never seen such destroyed heart, such ravagement of spirit on a person's face. I turned and walked away, realizing belatedly that there had been a scrawny baby in the bundle.

I got as far as the corner before I could get myself stopped, or put my head in order. The baby didn't bother me. The baby didn't matter. It was the woman. I could not even put into thoughts what I was feeling. Most of us have defenses in our personalities. Usually, we have layer after layer of them. Even when we are dying, we can still put some last personality defense on our faces. This was a face from which the last, bottom layer of defense had been peeled like an onion.

I took the rest of the money I had with me, four thousand piastres, and walked back to her and put that in her hand with the other note. She did not even look at it, and raised her face again, and her face did not change. However much money it was, it would not be enough. She knew it, and I knew it. It might keep her going for a week, maybe even longer, that was all. Somewhere under her defenselessness some part of her seemed to be trying to tell me she appreciated my concern.

I walked away, wondering what kind of hope I'd hoped to give. There wasn't enough money to help her. Not now. The United States had not helped her. Neither had the French. The South Viets hadn't helped her, the North Viets hadn't helped her, the VC had not helped her. And what any of them or all of them might do for future generations would not do her any good at all.

She was all of Vietnam to me.

EPILOGUE

Hawaiian Recall

recall 4.a *Mil.* A call on the trumpet,
bugle, or drum, which calls soldiers
back to the ranks, camp, etc.

I hadn't planned it. But since I had to go on to New
York anyway, I checked the fare and found it cost
about fifteen dollars more to go on by Honolulu, than
to go back the way I had come, via Paris. I had not
been in Vietnam more than a week, before I knew I
was going to do it. And once I had made up my mind,
it seemed I had known all along that I would go. That
I could not not go. A sounding of Recall.

The song *Jamaica Farewell* was much in my mind
on the long trip from Saigon to Honolulu. It did not
exactly approximate my situation, but it spoke of islands, of island weather, of lost youth, of the sea, of

237

island populations, and I still thought about Hawaii that way.

I had left Honolulu in August of 1942, with elements of the 25th Division heading for Guadalcanal, a boy of twenty-one. I had not been back since. Before that, I had lived in Hawaii for three years, in the military, as an enlisted soldier. After The Great War II, I had spent four more years writing a novel about those three years. A not inconsiderable investment. Seven years.

The big Pan-Am 747 was only half full. After fifteen hours of it, passengers stretched out over banks of three and four seats. All of them were military personnel or military dependents leaving Vietnam. I myself was too keyed up to sleep.

The west coast of Oahu was intensely familiar as we approached it. I picked out Mt. Kaala in the Waianae Range. Then Barbers Point. Ewa Beach. Keahi Point, the Pearl Harbor entrance. Fort Kamehameha. They were all words as familiar to me as New York or Paris or Robinson, Illinois. Then we were low over Hickam Field, and I suddenly no longer knew where I was. Everything was built up, expanded, beyond my wildest imaginings. Even looking east toward Aliamanu Crater and the Tripler Army Medical Center, I did not recognize where I was. The plane landed. I got a taxi into town. And I still recognized nothing. Four-lane freeways. Six-lane freeways. Ritzy-looking modernistic restaurants. What I remembered as cane fields was now all housing development. It looked incredibly rich, after Vietnam.

No matter how fast you run, you can never catch up with the past. In the first place, the past is never the past when it is happening to you. Secondly, it rolls away from beneath you so slickly, so greasily, you have difficulty just staying on your feet. Sometimes you can get an inkling of it, when time seems to collapse, and you peer through a momentary hole in your future, and say, "Someday, I'll think back about this moment, and recall just exactly the way it was, and remember . . ." But you never quite do. And it never quite comes. When I first went there in 1939, the "Good Old Days" of Hawaii were 1910, or even 1920, when there were no transoceanic planes, and we did not have aircraft carriers, and there were no cars or almost none, and Honolulu traffic moved on clanging streetcars under the palms, slowly, leisurely, and one arrived only by ship, moving in slowly past Sand Island, to dock near the Aloha Tower, which was a "cultural" focal point then. In 1939 there was no way I could be a part of those "Good Old Days." And I had no way of knowing then that thirty years later my then-present would be the sweeter, quieter "Good Old Days" for 1973; that in pre-Pearl Harbor 1939 and '40 I was already living and participating in, without appreciating it, a leisurely non-jet, non-tourism, non-high-rise, non-international-airport Golden Age looked back on wistfully from 1973.

I had not been able to get into the old Royal Hawaiian, luxury symbol of my youth. So I was booked into the Sheraton-Waikiki, one of the new high-rise hotels that have sprouted in Waikiki, which was right next door to the Royal. When we pulled up to it on Kalakaua Avenue, I couldn't even find the old Royal. Then I saw its characteristic pink, off between the buildings. Most of its gardens were gone, to shops and airline offices and high-rise competition. It looked dwarfed and stunted among its neighbors. From my room on the twenty-fifth floor of the Sheraton I could look down on it, or down at the Sheraton pool, or off at Diamond Head and along the beach, or out to sea. The sheer richness of America was like a cold douche, after Saigon. I could have dwelt on this sourly, but after Saigon, and Hue, and Can Tho, I didn't feel sour. My social conscience didn't bother me at all. I was only animally grateful. The first thing I did was to have myself a real genuine American shower.

I decided the next thing to do was to hire myself a chauffeured car. It was eight-thirty in the morning and I hadn't been to bed in twenty-four hours but I could no more have slept than I could have flown. I had never driven in Honolulu. Only once or twice had I even had money enough to take a taxi—except for what we used to call "the jitneys," which took loads of us north to Schofield Barracks for fifty cents apiece after the last buses had left. There was a long line-up at the row of car-rental desks in the lobby.

There were two big conventions staying in the hotel, the beautiful half-white, half-Chinese girl told me, and I would have to wait forty-five minutes for my drivered car. I decided to use the time by having a drink at the beach bar of the Royal, and walked out to the street.

Only the Waikiki Theater and the Moana Hotel a half a block down were things I had ever seen before. I had difficulty finding the entrance to the Royal Hawaiian. Its profuse gardens had been cut down by sixty or seventy percent. The corner where Maggio had had his fist fight with the two MPs had disappeared completely. But once inside the entrance, I found I remembered, and that it looked about the same. The shops looked less expensive, though, and the lobby less formidably rich. It struck me forcibly suddenly, that I could walk into any of the shops and buy just about anything they had for sale. The beach patio had been changed and remodeled in some way I could not exactly define. Three huge jolly Hawaiian mama-sans joked along the tables with hotel clients they seemed to know. I bought my drink, a beer, drank it, and slunk back to the Sheraton. I remembered the times I had watched Air Force pilot officers drunk and fighting on the Royal Hawaiian's lawn after Midway—or was that Prewitt?

My driver was a young friendly hapa-Hawaiian who was maybe a third Japanese. When he turned his head and said, "Where do you want to go," I discovered I didn't know where I wanted to go. Some of the out-of-city places, like Schofield Barracks, Hanauma Bay, Makapuu Head, I was leaving till the next day and doing myself in a you-drive. But there were still lots of places in Honolulu proper I wanted to visit. But I found I could no longer remember many of the names.

Had I ever been in Hawaii? the driver wanted to know. His voice had the soft, slurring lilt that is so delicious in the Hawaiian English. I told him yes, I used to live there, a long time ago. In the War. Then I thought I better clarify, and cleared my throat. World War II, that is. "Well, you'll find us changed," he said. I could see his eyes watching me curiously in the mirror. Lamely, I told him to take me over into Kaimuki, the old Japanese section behind Diamond Head. There was a house up the hill I wanted to see there. But I couldn't remember the name of the street.

Did I mean Maunilani Heights? Yes, that was it.

The street ran straight up . . . Wilhelmina Rise? he said. That was it. That was where I wanted to go.

The house was the house of Prewitt's hooker girl-friend Alma. It wasn't on Wilhelmina Rise itself, but on a street just off it. I couldn't remember the name of the street. But when I saw it on the street sign, I remembered: Sierra Drive. I had the driver turn off on it and drive past the house.

Wilhelmina ran straight up, up and up arrow-straight, and from up here you could see the whole of Waikiki and downtown Honolulu. Prewitt's hooker Alma had never actually lived in the Sierra Drive house. I did not know who had lived there. I had never been inside it. I had had a hooker girlfriend myself, who had served somewhat as the model for Alma and had lived not far away, and I had chosen the house for Alma myself because of having passed it so many times and having wanted to live there. I saw the driver's eyes watching me curiously in the rearview mirror again, and told him to take me downtown to the Army-Navy Y on Hotel Street.

If the house on Wilhelmina Rise was a sort of aching thrill to see again, the Army-Navy Y and Hotel Street area was the ache with the thrill excised. The whole area looked like some sort of ghost town. When I asked the driver, he said it had been like that for a long time. There were still some girls around at night, but they were pretty low types. I could do a lot better out near Waikiki. His car was free for the night, if I wanted to hire him.

It was amazing. The area had once been a swarm-ing hive of bars, street vendors, tattoo parlors, shoot-ing galleries, photo galleries, market shops, fruit and vegetable shops, and hooker joints occupying the rooms upstairs and labeled hotels. Now there was hardly a soul on the streets, and most of the shops and bars were shuttered and closed. Once it had been our Mecca, toward which we rose and prayed every morning, before Reveille. Compressed into a half-mile area down by the docks between the King's Palace and the little river, and bursting at the seams to break out, it had been the bottomless receptacle of our dreams and frustrations, and of our money. The payday payroll. Now it was all coming down soon, the driver said, and an urban reclamation would be built in its place.

I had him drive me around the old streets. I had forgotten most of their names. I had remembered King St. and Hotel St. But I had forgotten Fort St., Bishop St., Bethel St., Union St., Queen Emma St., Adams St. I had even forgotten Beretania St. and Nuuanu Ave. I looked at the corner bar, now closed, where Warden had come hunting for Prewitt when Prewitt was AWOL. The old Wu Fat's Chinese Restaurant was still there, still open, on its corner but it had not been repainted in a long time and its bright Chinese colors looked drab. The driver said it was coming down, too. Wu Fat's was where Maggio had begun his final rampage that ended in his going to the Stockade. Right next door to it had been the streetdoor entrance to the New Senator Hotel (I called it New Congress) where Alma worked. I saw the driver watching me again curiously in the mirror, and told him to take me past the Aloha Tower at the foot of Fort St., and then drive me back out to Waikiki to the Sheraton.

One of the biggest single differences was that in the old Hawaii the tourist business was incidental to a way of life, and that now the way of life was incidental to the tourist business. You saw this all over the island. The next morning, when I went down for my you-drive car, I found I had to take a hotel bus from the Sheraton back down Kalakaua almost to Ala Moana to pick up my little Dodge at a large house trailer converted into an office in a filling station parking lot. The two conventions and an unexpected influx of tourist parties had overtaxed the hotel's delivery service. The little bus was packed with families and quartets of couples, all going to pick up cars, and they had accents from all over the US. They had traveled, and rented cars, just about all over the world, and the wryly humorous complaints I heard about the bus showed they knew their way around.

It was good not to have someone eyeing me in the rearview mirror. Strangely enough, I felt a little like a man going off full of nervous guilt to meet some clandestine call girl or mistress. I planned to visit Hanauma Bay first, out of town out Kalanianaole Highway beyond Diamond Head at the foot of Koko Head. Hanauma Bay was where Prewitt was trying to get when he was killed on the Waialae Golf Course, which I drove past in a few minutes. Hanauma Bay was where the confrontation between Warden and Stark over Karen Holmes happened, and Stark chopped up his kitchen tent with his cleaver. Hanauma Bay had been my company's command post for almost a year after Pearl Harbor, until we left for Guadalcanal. After Hanauma Bay, I planned to drive the six miles on out to our old beach position at Makapuu Head, where I had spent so many isolated weeks. I had written one of my best short stories, *The Way It Is,* about Makapuu. Later, I had written a whole novel, *The Pistol,* with Makapuu as the principal setting. Then, in the afternoon, I was going to drive up to Schofield Barracks.

I could not help but feel I owned a small piece of all of them. A piece no real-estate agent could sell from under me.

But I did not get beyond Hanauma Bay that morning. By the time I left Hanauma Bay it was too late to go on, unless I wanted to miss my date at Schofield that afternoon. I hadn't meant to stay that long. I had driven up over the Koko Head saddle, and the blind V-shaped side-road cutoff to Hanauma was there just exactly as it had always been, except that now it was blacktopped. At the foot of it down the hill you ran in under the same canopy of thorn trees and longleaf pine over the bare soil. The old popcorn wagon from before the war, that we had made our CP field-telephone center, was no longer there. But the weathered clapboard GENTS and LADIES buildings we had used indiscriminately, one on either side of the road, were still there. I spotted in my mind's eye where Warden's —where our—CP tent had been, and on the other side of the road where Stark's kitchen tents had sat. I had never known a 1st/Sgt named Warden, and had never known a Mess/Sgt named Stark. It was confusing. Some new picnic tables and benches of concrete had been spotted around.

The parking lot was full of cars. New ramparts of field stone had been built along the edge of the forty-foot cliff, and a new auto road that had not been there before had been built down its face to the beach. I walked down. On the beach the old clapboard pavilion I remembered, where one of the key scenes between Pfc Mast and a Cpl named Winstock had taken place in *The Pistol,* had been torn down and replaced with a modernistic reinforced-concrete monstrosity. The old pavilion had had a dining room, but the new building had none. Hamburgers and chiliburgers were dispensed at a window. There seemed to be more palm trees on the grass than I remembered, but none of the longleaf pine trees seemed to be any bigger. Families of tourists and local picnickers in trunks and bikinis sunbathed on the grass or lay on the sand beach. Swimmers trumpeted and cavorted in the shallow water between the beach and the shallow reef just offshore.

In our day, after the War began, there was nobody. Deserted. The pavilion locked up. We had strung barbed wire all along the beach. Our company commander had got permission to put a gate of concertina in the wire, so we could swim. But without girl swimmers it had been much less fun, and gradually we had all but stopped.

I sat a long time on the grass. I was uncomfortable. I seemed to keep wanting to look around for something else to appear, or occur. Finally I put on my brand-new trunks and went to the spot where our concertina gate had been and waded out and swam to the reef. Even without a mask I could see the reef was exactly the same as I remembered. The hole we had blasted in it to enlarge the swimming area was still there. I swam back to the beach and lay on the grass, still wanting to keep looking around for something. I got dressed and ate a chiliburger, sitting on the raised concrete porch of the "new" building. Young kids yelled and pushed each other and played around me and down on the grass. Suddenly, without any preparation at all, tears were up behind my eyes. All that blood, all that sweat. How many men? Tears for thirty years, gone somewhere. Tears for a young idiotic boy in a "gook" shirt and linen slacks. It was after one o'clock when I pulled the car back up onto the V-shaped cutoff, and too late to go to Makapuu.

There was now a four-lane highway all the way to Schofield Barracks, but first you had to extricate yourself from all the freeways around Honolulu and Pearl Harbor. Once I was safely on Route 99 north and could look at the country, I could see that just about everywhere the pineapple fields I remembered had diminished and urban housing developments had increased. But when I went through the Main Gate—where the MP on duty hardly gave me a glance—everything looked the same as it had looked thirty years before. I might have moved backward in time. The main flagpole was the same pure white. The Post Library was the same building, in the same place. I turned right at the proper point, and drove down along the front of the four Infantry quadrangles that I knew so well, one of which I had lived in for two years. They had not been changed. I knew every shelf on the inside of the Post Library, too. It was there I had first picked up Thomas Wolfe's *Look Homeward, Angel,* and heard some "mystic" call telling me I was a writer. I wondered if they had changed the inside. I had called the Post PR officer the day before, and been given a number to call when I arrived. But I put off calling. I drove around the streets of the Post, remembering this, remembering that. There was lots I did not remember. Mainly, the beauty. Schofield Barracks is probably the most beautiful post the US Army has, or ever had. I had not remembered it. Long stretches of green lush lawn, with short palms and tall palms and spreading hardwoods thrusting up here and there out of its rolling expanses. I had not remembered it because I had never noticed it much. Had I not been too preoccupied, there were a lot of things on the Post I might have enjoyed. And back-dropping it all, what I always thought of as The Pregnant Woman—Kole Kole Pass in the Waianae Range to the west. You could see her breasts, Mt. Kaala the highest point was her belly, Waianae Peak her knees, Peacock Flats her shins, and the cut at the pass made her long flowing hair, dropping straight from a jutting face-shaped ridge. She had always haunted me, and from up close, inside the confines of the Post, she haunted me anew. Immutable as the Post itself seemed immutable, she loomed over it no matter where you stood, no matter where you looked, re-minding every soldier of the feminine. A cruel sculpture to be perpetually confronted by. I drove three times around the old Post Theater, also still un-changed, and its V-shaped parking lot with the old roofed-over open-air bus station for Honolulu at the bottom, catercorner to my old 27th Infantry quadrangle. Scene of so many lonely evenings thirty years before, when I had the money. I saw it had a James Garner movie playing. And found myself on Kole Kole Pass Road, headed toward the hills, and let the car run on, carrying me there.

I had marched in formation out that road so many times. Hoarse voices counting cadence. Up past the baseball diamond to the empty field beyond for close-order drill. On up, past the golf course for squad and platoon small-unit tactical problems. Beyond that were the ranges set against the hills—rifle, mortar, artillery. Danger-warning signs, though newer, still invited passers-by to stay on the road. Then as the road steepened and began to snake, climbing to the pass, I passed the old Stockade rock pile, hollowed into an amphitheater back into the mountainside. Overgrown with grass and weeds, it clearly had fallen into disuse. I had wanted to see that place, again.

At the top of the pass I got out, and talked with the chubby Marine guard from the Naval Ammunition Depot in the Waianae Valley down the other side, and stood looking off over Waianae Valley to the sea, and looked back down at the Post spread out on the plateau behind me. I had once marched up to Kole Kole alone—twice; two times—with a full field pack and an escorting noncom, over some stupid argument with my company commander. I had used the incident on Prewitt in the novel, and it had been reproduced in the film version. Now I no longer knew whether Prewitt had done it, or I had. After a while, I got back into the car.

I called the Post PR Office from an outdoor phone booth under the open-shed roof of the bus station in the theater parking lot. One of the phone booths had an OUT OF SERVICE sign on it. Under it some sour graffitist had lettered, "Don't you wish you were!"

I knew that once the other people came into it, it would change. But there was no way out of that. If I did not call, I could not visit the installations I wanted. It was nobody's fault. But once the PR people arrived, the past went out of it. Vanished in thin air. Disappeared. It was as though I held a tenuous cord in my hand, that could not survive conversations and references and talk about itself, and the interplay of

personalities. It became a typical, polite, convivial
visit of a writer to a modern Army post, 1973. I was
taken to a scheduled parade of the division's service
battalions, and introduced to the 25th Division commander, a young major general. I chatted with some
of the officers' wives. Then I was taken to the division's Administrative Hq Company. The colonel there
gave me an elaborately formal pass, as a half joke,
entitling me to visit everything. I was taken up
beyond the golf course to a new building, to visit one
of the division's new Air Cav outfits. The "New Army"
was everywhere much in evidence. A great store was
set on the four-man barracks cubicle, as against the
wide, open bays with rows of bunks as in my day. It
was certainly pleasanter, more homelike. Finally, I
was taken to the Hq Building of the 2nd Battalion,
27th Infantry—my old outfit—housed in my old 27th
Regiment quadrangle.

It was into here that I had wanted to get, on my trip
to Schofield. And it was here that would be—I thought
—the culminating experience of my return. For two
years this old quadrangle had been my home. I had
slept on the second floor of the old 2nd Battalion barrack, which faced the Hq Building across the quadrangle square. Nowadays, in the modern streamlined
division, which carried within it its own helicopter
air transport, only one battalion of the regiment remained in active service. The other two were deac-
tivated. And if the old quad had seemed the same on
the outside, driving past, it was not the same inside.
In the corner of the interior square the old regimental
bandstand, which had also served us as a ring for the
regimental boxing smokers, was gone. And most of
the grass was gone. Trucks were parked everywhere,

and men worked on them. In one corner a volleyball game was in progress on the packed earth. And the ground floor of our old 2nd Battalion barracks, which once housed the orderly rooms and mess halls for the four companies, was now one huge, nicely done, modern mess hall for the entire organization. There were other changes.

But when we came off the stairs onto the second floor of the Hq Building—despite the other people present—for a moment the past appeared again. Absolutely nothing had changed here. The walls and doors were still painted the same horrible cream-green, and the polished old concrete floor still gleamed. They might never have been repainted since my day. The regimental trophy room was in the same place. The administrative offices were the same. And the colonel commanding's office down at the end was the same, his desk in the identical same place, the US and regimental flags behind his desk in their same stands. The only thing missing was the guard orderly's desk outside the colonel's office. I had sat at the desk the morning of Pearl Harbor, carrying messages for distraught officers, wearing the pistol I was later able to get away with. The initial sequence of *The Pistol* had taken place right here on this floor. But was it Pfc Richard Mast who had been here, or was it me? Or was it still a third unnamed, unnameable person? Where had it all gone? I kept waiting for something to appear, to happen. For a moment I felt actively dizzy.

Later, the young colonel walked me across the square to show me the new mess hall. Everything that could be done had been done to make eating pleasanter and more enjoyable, although, to me, the troopers didn't appear any less disgruntled. The young colonel had been a boy in grade school here back in 1940 when I had served here, his father an artillery officer. So had his adjutant. They grinned and he said he thought maybe I had been a little hard on the old folks. In any case, the old caste system was gone. You couldn't *make* these youngsters do anything, you had to explain to them what you wanted them to do, and make them understand it, and then lead them. I had heard pretty much the same thing all over Vietnam. We talked a bit about the "New Army." The two officers took me upstairs to the second floor, and I stood in the spot where my old bunk had been. The second floor here had not yet been remodeled into the four-man cubicles, and the bunks stretched in rows across the width and length of the barrack floor. I thought it looked considerably cooler, this way. I stood and looked down at my old bunk. Nobody came in through the open doors that I knew.

On our way back to the Hq Building the young colonel hollered at two troopers who were out washing their car in the barracks street. "I've got one down here that could stand a little polish, when you're through there," he called. The two soldiers grinned. "Yeah? Why don't you grab a sponge and come help with this one?" was the answer that came back. The colonel grinned and winked at me.

Later, I went with a young sergeant who wrote for the Schofield paper, to meet some of the unhappy types, the malcontents, whom he knew and had worked with. There were five of them sitting around a four-man cubicle, playing cards on a blanket on the floor around a candle. The lights had been turned off. All but one of them wore mustaches, and all of them had hair longer than was usual. Their complaints, when the sergeant got them down to bare rock, were primarily that they wanted to wear their hair and their mustaches even longer. Why, I asked. "So we won't look so much like soldiers," one of the boys said glumly. "The girls here don't like soldiers." Mainly, it came out, they did not like the Army because they were so lonely. In thirty years the song had changed almost not at all. The past seemed to rise up and roar at me like a wind tunnel.

We talked about the Stockade. The new Stockade. They did not appear to be afraid of it, as we had been. Apparently it had been moved from its old environs, down closer in the Post proper, and now consisted of a rather pleasant area surrounded by a white picket fence, like a cottage. It appeared to be run on a semi-honor system. The young PR sergeant offered to take me to see it, but added that it was rather late. There were only about seven guys there, working out summary courts, he said, and grinned. It was not like the old days. So instead we had some beer one of the boys had brought in, and talked about the Army. It was long after dark when I pulled the little car out onto the main road—past the MPs at the main gate, who did not even glance at me—and started back to Honolulu.

The next morning I drove out to Makapuu Head, which I had missed the day before. I was leaving that same night, and something kept telling me I shouldn't miss Makapuu. It too had played a very important part in my life, particularly after the War began. It had been at once the largest, the most primitive, and the most extended beach position of my company headquarters at Hanauma Bay. Being so far away, the food that got out to us there three times a day was always cold. There was no way to avoid it. I had spent over three months there after the War began.

Makapuu Head lay at the easternmost corner of Oahu. The main mountain range, the Koolau Range, ended there. And once you had turned that corner, you were on what was called the Windward Side of Oahu, where the sea wind blowing in from the east never stopped. In both the story *The Way It Is* and the novel *The Pistol,* I had used that never ceasing wind as a conscious symbol of pressure on the men.

It was five or six miles from the Hanauma Bay cutoff, and almost all of the way bulldozers and earth-moving equipment were at work on either the land-scape or the highway or both. The Lunalilo Freeway was obviously being extended this way, and the development was following it. The farms and cattle ranges I remembered had almost totally disappeared. I arrived at Makapuu depressed.

The Koolau Range ended at Makapuu in a huge cliff several hundred feet high. The old Kalanianaole Highway had been constructed down this cliff, leading to Waimanalo and Kaneohe. At the top of the fall there had always been a scenic overlook, out over Rabbit Island and the sea, where cars could park. Even in my day. But in my day, with the War, no cars had come. We had wished they would, knowing already that they couldn't, were not allowed. Now a steady stream of them arrived, as tourists pulled up, parked, got out to look, and then drove on.

But when I walked away from them and the constantly starting and stopping cars, on out onto the desolate little flat to seaward of the road, which further away led onto the destitute crags of Makapuu Point, they seemed to be no longer there. With the so-familiar, hard buffeting unceasing east wind in my face, I could no longer hear them in their protected spot. A curtain had dropped behind me, cutting me off from them, and with a kind of frightened, awed wonder I stood looking at a scene that had not changed one grass blade since I had last looked at it thirty years before. In front of me the thin soil covered with outcrops rose to the craggy cliffs of the Point. Not one outcrop had been disturbed. To the south looking out over the fall of land from the pass to the Kaiwi Channel, I could see the squared-off cleared spaces we had made to pitch our tents, all still there, exactly as we had made them. Everywhere around were the paths our feet and our picks had made, still faintly visible in the sparse grass. The only things missing were the men, and the tents themselves. And for a few moments every now and then from the corners of my eyes I thought I could see both —the men moving, the tents blowing, translucent like ghosts.

It is hard to give a full picture of the acute desolation of that place. The rocks are black and sharp and are everywhere, jutting up or just under the thin surface. Mostly it's because of that hard-flowing wind that never stops howling.

In November of 1941 my company had with our bare hands, and the aid of seven gasoline-driven jackhammers that would not shut off like pneumatic drills when you moved them, dug five pillboxes in the virgin rock up there, on those cliffs, and had floored them and walled them and roofed them, and apertured them, with concrete. Only one of them was visible from the road, and to see that one you had to know where it was. On December 7th we had been moved down here in trucks and occupied them with nothing but the machineguns and our rifles. And one canteen of water per man. I could no more not go look at them than I could have flown home via Honolulu without a stopover. My feet started carrying me up the complex of faded paths as surely as though they knew the way before my eyes did.

They were all there. All five of them. Somebody at some point had bricked the apertures shut, but most of them had been broken open. The hewn-rock stairs down into two of them had been blocked by rubble and trash, but by shouldering the steel doors of the other three I could get into those. I stood in each of them a long time, looking out and remembering times when late at night I had sat behind machineguns in all of them, staring out into the dark toward Rabbit Island and the beach that faced it.

When I came up out of the last one and started back down, I looked down and automatically placed my foot on a natural step in the rock that we had always used to climb in or out. It was still there, unchanged, uneroded, unchipped. And my foot still knew where it was. I stood staring down at it for several seconds, shocked, and when I looked back up and looked down the hill at the tourists and the clustered cars, it was as if I were back there in 1942, when the overlook was empty, peering forward into an unforeseeable future when it would be open and crowded with sightseers, as it was now. The only thing that was different was that I was alone, that there was nobody with me.

Foolishly, I began taking pictures. As if pictures

could capture what was happening to me. In a way I felt I was bearing witness—bearing the witness I had come back to Hawaii to authenticate. But just exactly what it was—except a thumbing of my nose at time —I didn't know.

That night an old friend drove me out to the airport to say good-by. We sat in the lounge and talked about the old days at the university in Manoa Valley, when I had gone there. But we ticketholders rode out to the plane in a bus, and I could not see the airport building to wave good-by. The airport itself looked entirely foreign. As tired as the others, I climbed the steep stairs. I had come back hoping to meet a certain twenty-year-old boy, walking along Kalakaua Avenue in a "gook" shirt, perhaps, but I had not seen him.